No one speaks more clearly than Joyce Hutchison and Joyce Rupp do about grief. They address hard questions in a gentle manner that brings hope and courage. Worth its weight in gold, this book shares a wealth of wisdom and comfort.

Rev. Dr. Deborah L. Patterson
Executive Director
Deaconess Parish Nurse Ministries, LLC
International Parish Nurse Resource Center

By combining storytelling with prayer and reflection, Joyce Hutchison and Joyce Rupp take us through the grieving process in both a unique and profound way. *Now That You've Gone Home* impacts the very soul of the reader because it is not only personal and real, but explores the depths of love one has for both the deceased and for the God who welcomes him or her Home.

Mauryeen O'Brien, O.P.
Author of *Gentle Keeping: Prayers and Services for Remembering Departed Loved Ones Throughout the Year*

If you are looking for a book that authentically, gracefully, and spiritually shares the stories of loss, the journey of grief, and God's compassionate healing touch, this book will exceed your expectations. A resource for grief support groups and the bereaved seeking a prayer-filled guide for their journey through grief.

Linda M Cherek, RN, MSW, LICSW, CT
Licensed Therapist and Bereavement Specialist
White Bear Lake, Minnesota

Joyce Hutchison and Joyce Rupp have done it again! The stories in *Now That You've Gone Home: Courage and Comfort for Times of Grief* offer affirmation, solace, and guidance for the many concerns and questions grievers experience. When we read the varied ways God's healing power has touched the lives of other grievers, it is easier to see our Beloved's presence in our own lives.

Dr. Nancy Reeves

Clinical psychologist, spiritual director, and author of *Gifts of the Eucharist: Stories to Transform and Inspire*

Now That You've Gone Home is as up close and personal as listening to a dear friend open her broken heart to you. As Joyce Hutchinson speaks to the reality of widowhood and invites others to share the challenges of grieving, Joyce Rupp reminds us of God's enduring love. This work of consolation and healing will be welcomed by the newly bereaved, those who minister to them, and hospice care specialists everywhere.

M. Donna MacLeod, RN, MSN

Author of *Seasons of Hope Guidebook: Creating and Sustaining Catholic Bereavement Groups* and *Seasons of Hope Participant Journals*

Now That You've Gone Home

Courage and Comfort
for Times of Grief

Joyce Hutchison

Joyce Rupp

ave maria press AmP **notre dame, indiana**

© 2009 by Ave Maria Press, Inc.

Founded in 1865, Ave Maria Press is a ministry of the Indiana Province of Holy Cross.

www.avemariapress.com

ISBN-10 1-59471-215-8   ISBN-13 978-1-59471-215-9

Cover image © Alamy Images.

Cover and text design by Katherine Robinson Coleman.

Printed and bound in the United States of America.

Library of Congress Cataloging-in-Publication Data

Now that you've gone home : courage and comfort for times of grief / [compiled by] Joyce Hutchison and Joyce Rupp.
     p. cm.
  ISBN-13: 978-1-59471-215-9 (pbk.)
  ISBN-10: 1-59471-215-8 (pbk.)
 1. Bereavement--Religious aspects--Christianity. 2. Grief--Religious aspects--Christianity. I. Hutchison, Joyce. II. Rupp, Joyce.
  BV4905.3.N69 2009
  248.8'66--dc22

                                                        2009019660

To all those significant persons

who have been a part of our lives

and have gone Home before us.

CONTENTS

BY JOYCE RUPP

As much as we desire those we love to remain with us forever, life continually changes. Nothing is permanent. One of the biggest changes in life comes when someone we cherish leaves us through death. With this loss comes an anguish that robs us of joy and destroys our inner peace. When this kind of change happens, we enter into a mourning period in which grief accompanies us every step of the way.

In our first co-authored book, *May I Walk You Home,* Joyce Hutchison and I presented stories and prayers to encourage and strengthen caregivers of the very ill. In our second book, *Now That You've Gone Home*, we again bring stories and prayers. This time we offer them to anyone who has experienced the loss of a loved one, with the hope of easing their sorrow and supporting their process of mourning.

As the two of us wrote this book, I was astounded at how the lives of my friends mirrored some of the stories you are about to read. I listened to the heartache of a new widow whose husband did not make it through surgery, the sadness of a woman whose sister died of Lou Gehrig's disease, the sorrow of a mother whose son took his own life, and the shock of a colleague whose longtime friend was killed in a car accident. As I heard their pain, I found myself constantly wishing this book was already in print so they could find comfort in knowing their responses to grief are similar to others who grieve, that they would know they are not alone in how they experience their loved one's departure.

In the following stories, Joyce Hutchison honestly and vulnerably shares her personal journey with grief, along with the other fifteen persons who relate their encounters with death. While each person's account of loss and ensuing grief is unique, there are numerous commonalities that weave through the narratives. As you read the stories in *Now That You've Gone Home*, you will notice that mental and emotional distress is a natural part of grief's predictable (and unpredictable) visitation.

The stories in this book are meant to sustain, comfort and encourage you. They are reminders that you do not travel your road of grief in isolation. At this very moment, others also bear the heavy weight of loss. They, too, know the suffering that grieving brings. This book will not take away the effects of your loss, but it can console your pain and assure you that your response to grief is natural and that it will not stay forever.

Now That You've Gone Home includes an array of stories, with varied aspects of the implications and complications of grief. We not only bid farewell to the one we love but we do so within the social context of others. The expansiveness of grief reaches into these relationships, into past woundedness and dashed dreams. Grief can challenge our ability to forgive, to accept a new way of living, to let go of guilt and regrets, to heal old hurts and anything else that holds us back from peace of mind and heart.

What lies beyond physical death remains a mystery for those of us who are left behind. Both Joyce Hutchison and I believe that physical death does not close the door to our connection with our loved ones. Love has the last word. It keeps the door open. Those we hold dear leave a part of themselves with us when they return to their eternal Home. As they move on to partake of the one Great Love that unites us all, the love they leave with us as they depart remains forever in our hearts.

Because it is often difficult to concentrate and to feel a sense of this Great Love's presence during times of grief, I have created brief meditations and prayers following each story. I have tried to respect every belief system while, at the same time, suggesting ways and words to unite with the One Love ever present with us.

We cannot hurry anyone through their grief, but *Now That You've Gone Home* can assist you to grieve, to have confidence in your ability to survive this tough part of your life and to be healed of the pain that has come with your significant loss. Life will not remain the same. The death of a loved one leaves an indelible mark on your life, but you can discover how to go on, how to "make a life" again without this beloved person in it. Cling to this hope. Trust that, with time, the best of your memories will turn into golden reservoirs of comfort and consolation.

ACKNOWLEDGMENTS

As the two of us reflect on how this book took shape and came to life, we are deeply grateful to those who influenced and contributed to its unfolding, to those who supported us in our efforts and affirmed our understanding of grief, especially the following persons: Faye Petersen, Dr. Tim and Michelle Vermillion, Linda Carey, Lisa Leimer, Mary Rose Stone, Vicki Vanderkwaak, Martha Kraber, Margaret Pommer, Janece Rohwer, all of those wonderful women friends who call themselves *The Playhouse Group*, and the *Morning Midwives* who gather with us to pray and cheer us on.

We are grateful to those who graciously shared their experiences with us after their loved ones left them behind, knowing it would be painful for them to go back into their memories of grief: Mikayla Bennett, Janet Bennett, Susie Flood, Nan Gaul, Barbara Hans, Mary Jones, Diane Kelly, Julie Lisac, John McCann, PJ McDonald, Catherine McEniry, Marilyn Mullin, Rodney Spence, Katie Swalwell, and Karen Tandy.

The skilled care and compassionate presence that we witnessed in hospice personnel, chaplains, social workers, volunteers, grief counselors, home health aides, and family caregivers of the dying continually inspired us. How blessed we have been by these wonderful persons.

Thank you to all those at Ave Maria Press who assisted us in our publishing endeavor.

~ Joyce Hutchison and Joyce Rupp

My family was an important part of writing this book. Dick Spidle (whose wife died in 2003), and I reconnected at our high school reunion. He and I were married on December 29, 2006. His daughters (Jane and Janet) and their families are supportive of this new relationship, while knowing that no one can take their mother's place. My husband died twelve years before Dick and I married, so my children (Joe, Mike, and Julie) and their families were further down the road with their grief . They were also supportive, even though it is still difficult to see someone in the other parent's place. Their openness to this new relationship and their ability to share our grief of the past and our joy of the present have been a generous gift from all of them. Dick and I are grateful for the opportunity to share the remainder of our life's journey together. There are thirteen beautiful grandchildren, Emma, George, Margaret, Griffin, Garrett, Ruby, Mose, Lila, Anabel, Samantha, AJ, Mikayla and Derek, who shared in the grief of having a grandparent die but who now bring so much fun and anticipation to our lives.

~ Joyce Hutchison

BY JOYCE HUTCHISON

The painful journey of grief changes us in ways that no other experience can. Sorrow is not something we seek, yet this unwanted visitor of death manages to find its way inside our deepest self. Grief actually holds the possibility of enriching our lives. Experiencing our grief, and allowing ourselves to truly be with it, creates an openness for compassion to grow stronger in us. Of course, it is impossible for us to believe this when our heart contains an immense amount of sadness. I only know this truth of grief's potential by looking back to where this unwanted visitor took over my life time and again.

Let me share how grief paid me numerous visits. My grandmother Griffin died when I was in the eighth grade. I was closer to her than any other person in my life, except my twin brother. We were good "buddies." I don't remember a lot about how I grieved, but I remember feeling lost without her. I believed she loved me more than anyone else in this world. Grandma was the one I could ask my most important questions, and she was the one I laughed with the most. She had terminal cancer the last months of her life and she lived at our house. I loved to help her take a bath, get a wet washcloth for her dry lips, or just sit with her. Even though she couldn't talk and she slept a lot, I loved just sitting with her. I was sure Grandma knew I was there and that thought comforted me.

When I was twenty-two my twin brother Joe was killed in a car accident. I had only been married to Gary for three months and I did not stop to grieve Joe's death. Instead, I stuffed my feelings away inside of me as much as possible. Joe and I were always close and even knew what each other was thinking. We shared our thoughts and ideas with each other, but did so privately. I think we didn't want to let anyone know how connected we were because we felt they wouldn't understand. Joe would tell me when he was in trouble and I would try to help him. In turn, he was very protective of me. The deep love between us made it too difficult for me to face the painful loss when he died so young.

It wasn't until twenty-two years later, when I was forty-four, that I began to truly grieve Joe's death. This was the day my mom died of cancer. I felt like Joe died that day, too. I've learned that grief never just goes away, it simply waits on us to recognize the loss. One day, there grief is, insisting that we take time with the hidden pain of our goodbye. I was sad for my mom and for my twin brother at the same time. My greatest comfort was that they were now together, because Mom had really never gotten over Joe's death. I spent a lot of quiet time just thinking about them and allowing myself to feel how much I missed them.

The next time grief paid a visit, I was unprepared. My husband Gary had been diagnosed with cancer in 1970, when I was twenty-nine. His physicians told us that, with treatment, he had six months to live. Gary lived twenty-four more years after that. In those twenty-four years, he experienced two primary cancers, a colostomy, numerous bouts of chemo and radiation therapy, and heart bypass surgery twice. He was in and out of the hospital numerous times. He died on June 7, 1994, after the second heart surgery. I was fifty-four.

My oldest brother Ed died in January 2000 after a five-year battle with a neuromuscular disease that caused him to be bedbound and unable to walk, talk, swallow, or move his extremities. A year later, my dad died at my home after a few months of declining health, a week before his ninetieth birthday. The following year in April 2002, my second-oldest brother, Rich, died of lung cancer. During the late stages of his illness, he was also in my home where I had the privilege of caring for him. My last living and youngest brother, Gene, died of lung cancer in May 2007.

I came from a family of seven, with my parents and my four brothers, and now I am the only one left. If someone had told me when I was twenty that this is what my life would contain, I would have protested, "No way! I can't deal with it." Well, I've changed my mind about that. As I look at life from my perspective now, I wouldn't change a thing. I would not have chosen to have death hold such a prominent place on my journey, but this road I have traveled has made me who I am today and I am grateful. Without experiencing the pain of my loss, I would lack understanding and empathy. I would not grasp what others are feeling or how it is for them to go through their losses. Because of the experiences I've had, I am more able to offer my compassion, understanding, and open heart to others. My encounters with grief have enabled me to "get into the skin of another," to empathize, to truly be "with them" in what they are feeling.

I recall a woman by the name of Karen whose husband died several years before Gary did. She walked with me through my passage of grief with a deep understanding that she could not have found in any other way. Her compassionate presence meant the world to me. In writing this book, I hope to assist others who have undergone the painful process of significant loss, as Karen assisted me. I want those who grieve to know that what they are feeling is part of a natural process, that they can survive when sorrow takes over their lives.

One of the helpful things I did during my grieving time, especially after Gary died, was to keep a journal. I look back on those journal entries now and find some of them a bit shocking, particularly the pages where I begged Gary over and over to come back. I knew in reality that it was impossible for him to return, but those entries show how irrational our minds can be when we are feeling extremely emotional and desperately alone. I wrote in my journal regularly for two years and sometimes went to the cemetery with journal and pen in hand. There I poured out my love for Gary and my overwhelming grief.

It was two years after Gary's death before I knew that I would be okay, before I believed I would survive. On the two-year anniversary of his death I went to the cemetery, sat beside his headstone (which also has my name on it), took off my wedding ring, and decided I had to move on. That day I wrote to each of my three children. I reminded them of the painful years of grief I had experienced and explained that, even though I continued to miss their dad tremendously, I had to finally begin to move forward. I assured them that I knew he would want me to live happily instead of continuing to wish him back. During those two years I had allowed myself to truly grieve, and even though I would always miss him, I knew then that I would be okay.

I did move on, gradually, but what amazes me is that fourteen years later, something I see, or something someone says, will trigger a memory or experience of Gary and grief stirs up in me again. When that happens, I let myself have a good cry while I remember all that I found dear about him.

Our loved ones will always be in our hearts. This truth came back to me time and again as I wrote the stories in this book. A lot of tears flowed as I recalled my loved ones who died and who live on in my heart. Writing about my loss and subsequent grief has been a difficult task and yet, by revisiting my grief and writing about it, I have taken another step in my personal growth toward healing and wholeness.

Each of us grieves and recovers in our own way and in our own time. Each of us also has some common experiences of grief. I hope this book touches your grief in a way that helps you move forward. May it also encourage you by finding kinship with others who have suffered loss, and seeing that they have been able to make it through what appeared to be unending heartache.

As you move through and beyond your grief, may your life become richer in kindness and deeper in understanding because of the experience you have had.

STORIES

OF GRIEF

BY

JOYCE HUTCHISON

CHAPTER ONE

How Can It Be

That You Have Died?

The first days after my husband died contained a whirlwind of activity. There was no way to focus on anything for more than a few seconds. I was a robot going through the motions of planning the funeral and greeting the many people who came to offer their condolences. It didn't seem possible that Gary was really gone. In my daze, I felt that if I just went through what had to be done, then it would all be over and we'd be back to normal. Surely I'd wake up in a few days and he would be home again. I could not comprehend the reality of his death. My mind didn't work well enough to try to sort it out. There wasn't the opportunity either, not with people around all the time as we prepared for his funeral. While I felt comforted by those who were in the house, I still could not take in the fact of Gary's death. None of what was going on made much sense.

My three adult children were with me and helped with countless plans and decisions. There was a lot of talking about their dad. We cried and even laughed as we remembered certain of his characteristics, like being late for events. Someone said that if Gary were alive, he would be late for his own wake service. In planning the funeral, we were able to talk about what was important to him and what he enjoyed. We set up a table at the service with some of his favorite things on it. The children chose his tools and calendar pocket books where he kept his lists for each day. I chose the television remote control—he surfed every channel several times during each program he watched, so as not to miss anything. We all decided to write him a letter and place it in either the casket or in his suit pocket, to tell him the things in our hearts we wanted and needed to say. The kids thought it was a great help to ease their sorrow. Writing my letter to Gary only temporarily helped with mine.

While there were endless tasks to get done, nothing seemed real. I went to bed at night and even slept a bit. Then I'd wake up to the nightmare going on around me. It was as if I were watching all of it from afar. Just a week ago I had been planning to bring him home from the hospital. My thoughts were often consumed with the last days and weeks of what happened: Gary had gone into the hospital less than two weeks before to have heart bypass surgery. He wasn't supposed to die during surgery, but he did. I kept asking: "How can this have happened?" I thought he would most likely die before me, but I never dreamed he would die when he did. He had a history of coming through serious medical situations before when it looked like he might not do so.

At the funeral, people spoke about Gary, recalling his empathy and compassion for others, how he reached out his hand to them in their time of need. I knew he was like that, but it was surprising to hear others say these wonderful things about him. While I remember little about the funeral, I do know that it was a meaningful event where the children were pleased and proud of their dad. There were so many people there, and yet I don't remember anyone who was there. In a way, I think I dreaded for the funeral to be over, because I didn't know what I would do next. At the same time, I wanted all of the commotion to stop, so maybe I could think again. Among the thousands of thoughts that went through my head, there came fleeting ones about the fact that I was going to be alone from then on. The thought quickly passed, but in the instant it was there, panic lurched in my stomach.

I had worked with hospice for many years and believed I knew everything about grief. After Gary died, it didn't seem like I knew anything. The morning after his death I remembered a woman whose husband died several weeks earlier in the hospice house where I was currently employed as the director. She was close to her husband and had been with him every minute until his death. She came to see the staff at hospice a week after he died to thank us for being so good to them. This new widow had the most painful, lost, and lonely look on her face. I remembered thinking, "The poor woman seems to have lost hope." In the moment of my own grief, I pictured her face and thought, "So *this* is what that painful face was about." I felt just as lost and miserable. It hit me then, that I hadn't known nearly as much about grief as I thought I did.

I had to figure out how to continue the journey set before me. The road was blurry. I asked God to walk beside me and help me take it just one step at a time, to pick me up when I stumbled. I knew the kids were leaving in a few days and I dreaded it. I didn't want them to know my fears, though, as it would be difficult enough for them. They were only in their twenties and I didn't want to interfere with their young lives. I wanted to be strong for them, as well as for myself. I knew I would be, because it was important; but, oh dear, I felt so weak. I had easily advised others to take one day at a time, but now I had to apply that advice to myself. I had no idea how hard it would be.

The part of my journey that I had to travel from this point forward was unknown. There were no roadmaps. My husband had gone Home and left me behind. There I was, asking, "Now that you've gone Home, how can I continue without you, Gary?"

Meditation

Find a place where you can have some uninterrupted quiet time. Although God may seem distant from you, this beloved presence is truly with you and desires to comfort you in your loss.

Hold in your hands a photo of your loved one who has died. Allow your thoughts and emotions to come forth as you look at this photo.

Visualize God's kindness and care caressing and comforting you like a warm ray of sunshine on a cold, turbulent day. Rest awhile in the warmth of this enduring love as you grieve your great loss.

Prayer

Tender-hearted God,
the one I love has gone to be with you
and I am left behind to mourn my loss.
I long for what can be no more.
Help me to continue my journey
without _____ as a part of my life.
Take my sorrow, emptiness, and heartache.
Soften it with your compassionate heart.
As I grieve the departure of my dear one,
hold me close in your loving care.

For Today

Each time I feel weak and think I cannot go
on, I will turn to God for assurance and
strength.

CHAPTER TWO

Nothing

about Life

Is Familiar

The following is a journal entry of mine a week after the funeral:

The kids went home a few days ago and this house echoes with silence, or maybe it echoes with "where is Gary?" I am really trying to manage each day but it is terribly difficult. I wonder if I can endure this. I have the most awful hurting in my chest and can hardly stand it. I have often heard the expression "heartache" but I didn't know I could actually feel something like this in my body. My heart aches so much it is sometimes difficult to breathe.

I now have all of the Thank You notes done and am getting dishes returned, but I continue to feel like I'm just going through the motions of life most of the time. I cry so much it seems like I don't have a tear left in me anymore. The strange thing is that all of the crying doesn't help because the ache in my chest is still there. Nothing about life makes me happy. I am so lonesome for Gary and find myself thinking he'll come back. I guess I know in my head that he can't come back, but in my heart he is going to be here one of these days.

Yesterday I received the death certificates and I'm trying to get them to insurance companies and take care of the financial business. It is meaningless but necessary work. I sometimes wonder if I will be able to survive okay financially, but because my mind is so foggy, this concern doesn't stay with me long.

That might partly be because I don't care. How can there be a future that means anything without Gary? I do care about the kids and I want to live for them, but at the same time I wonder how I can live the rest of my life without him. I never dreamed I could miss anyone this much.

People call to inquire about how I am doing and to say they are thinking of me. I tell them I'm doing okay because there are no words to tell them how horrible the grief and loss is. I don't think they could possibly understand.

A few days ago, I started back to work and that is a struggle. Being in charge of a hospice house involves so much responsibility. No matter what tasks I have ahead of me, the loudest thing in my head is that Gary is dead. It drowns out every other thought. I find it difficult to concentrate or to keep a thought in my mind long enough to complete a task or deal with the issue at hand. I am trying to cope the best I can and just hope my mind will work better with time.

Being at the bedside of the dying has always been a spiritually peaceful place for me. Now even that does not seem comfortable. I just keep seeing Gary and I want to run away from everything. I have to really focus on this lack of concentration because this is my work and has always been my passion. I have to believe that time will help. I feel like I am living in another country, unable to speak the language. Life doesn't make any sense right now.

Nothing is familiar and I can't remember anything. When I leave work, I sometimes don't remember driving home. I hope I stopped at the red lights and stop signs but I have no recollection of the drive. It is so scary and I pray that God takes care of me. Will my mind ever work again as it used to? My thoughts scatter here and there and many of them collide in my mind at the same time. I also have no interest in anything. Nothing else matters except that Gary is gone. Please don't let me lose my mind; or do I even care if I do? I don't know what I think. I have to hang on for my children. They would be devastated if both parents were gone. God, please walk with me and keep me safe. I feel like I am hanging on by a tiny thread, barely able to survive.

Meditation

Choose a place, either indoors or outdoors, where you can walk unhurriedly for at least ten minutes. Take slow, easy steps. As you walk, be attentive to your breath.

On your in-breath, breathe in the courage and strength that God offers to you.

On your out-breath, breathe out the pain and distress that you are experiencing.

Let your worries and concerns be put aside. All you need to do is walk and breathe, walk and breathe, walk and breathe.

Prayer

Enduring Presence,
draw me close to you when I doubt my ability
to make it through this painful time of loss.
Strengthen me when I fear I'll fall apart.

Steady me when I lose my inner balance.
Clear my confused mind. Ease my aching heart.
Help me have the willpower to do what must be done.
I need to know you are near and will not leave me.
More than ever before, I am turning to you in faith,
with confidence that your love will not fail me.

For Today

I will focus only on the present moment so
my mind can hold just one thing at a time.
When fear of falling apart seizes me, I'll
pause, breathe in as fully as I can, and then
let my breath out slowly.

CHAPTER THREE

This House

Has Never Been

So Empty

After my husband's death one of the most difficult things was coming home to an empty house after work and having to walk in the door. I had never come home to an empty house before. Gary was either home because of health issues or, when he was working, always got home before I did. After he died, I would pull in to the driveway and dread going into the house. It was almost as if there was a huge monster in there. The emptiness and the loneliness truly did feel that way. Physical exercise helped me cope, so I quickly changed my clothes after work and went for a brisk three-mile walk each day. I often cried while I was walking and that helped me feel better and cope with life a bit better.

Those wonderful stress-relieving endorphins that my body released with my activity brought more comfort and peacefulness than I could have imagined. Hope arose in me and stayed longer after those walks than at any other time during the day. The relief often lasted only a few hours though and by 7:00 p.m. I started feeling low again and would go out for another two- mile walk. I often thought that releasing endorphins by walking must be like taking a antidepressant because of how much better I felt.

Eating alone was as difficult as coming home to the empty house. After I fixed myself something to eat, I sat in front of the television so I could think about something else besides the fact that no one was there with me. I had never eaten alone or lived by myself in my entire life. First there was my birth family of seven, then a nurse's dorm of a hundred-plus women in training, and then my marriage. When Gary died, I felt like my house doubled in size. The silence was deafening. A feeling of desperation sometimes took over me. I would find myself walking through the house crying, at times even yelling for Gary to come back. I knew my thinking was irrational, but I couldn't stop it. During those times, I felt as if I was looking for Gary and could not find him. I would sit in his chair in the evening so that I wouldn't have to look at its absolute emptiness. This may sound strange but I think sitting there helped me feel less miserable.

We had a golden retriever, Hannah, who was a wonderful help to me in my desolation. Hannah did plenty of her own grieving because she was Gary's faithful companion. I didn't realize dogs grieved until I saw how she lay at the foot of his chair and wouldn't move. When I sat in Gary's chair and cried, she put her paws up on the arm of the chair and licked my tears. It was as if Hannah, in her sadness, also felt my pain. Her companionship provided a much-needed gift. Hannah brought life to the desolate house, and she also went on my walks, keeping me moving briskly.

One of the biggest challenges was sleeping in our bed. I tried it several times and, no matter what I tried, couldn't go to sleep. I kept thinking I could hear Gary's footsteps coming up the stairs, and I would lie there listening for him. I slept on the sofa in the family room for over a year. Sometimes I think I was a bit afraid upstairs and felt safer on the main floor but, as I reflect back on those days, I wonder if the biggest reason I slept on the sofa was that it made Gary's absence seem temporary. Something in me pretended that I would just sleep on the sofa until he came back. That is how the mind can work when grief consumes our entire self.

When I woke up, sometimes quite early, I longed to go back to sleep. I couldn't bear facing another day. My thoughts always rested on the question: "Will today be as difficult as yesterday?" Many different feelings and challenges lay before me each day. I had to learn how to manage these daily ordeals, each of which held something bigger and more painful than I could possibly have realized before Gary's death. I don't believe there is any way to be fully prepared for the agonizing experience of grief. Each day I begged God to walk beside me and keep me from falling apart.

Meditation

Sit in a comfortable chair. Hold an empty bowl in your hands.

Reach into the bowl with one of your hands and feel how hollow and empty the space is. Look at the outside of the bowl. Notice how it holds the emptiness and provides a container for it.

Close your eyes and visualize God's compassion as the container for your grief and loneliness. Inside you feel empty, but an invisible presence is holding your emptiness with the strong container of loving kindness.

Let yourself be held in this Love.

Prayer

Comforting One,
inside of me there's a huge cavern of loneliness.
I don't think my heart can be more empty than it is.
Each part of my daily routine cries out with sorrow.
Every day is an endless stretch of persistent grief.
Teach me how to care for myself amid this pain.
Grant me courage to do this as best I can,
especially when I feel as though I will fall apart.
May I be patient with my unwanted emotions
and trust that one day my inner world will change.

For Today

Whenever I see an object that is empty, I will
remember that the strong container of God's
love holds my emptiness.

CHAPTER FOUR

Will Life

Ever Be Normal

Again?

Four months after Gary's death, some things had become easier. I was able to come home and walk into the house without the devastating fear that I wouldn't survive my loneliness. Even so, the house continued to be dauntingly quiet and empty. Before he died, Gary was often asleep on the sofa when I arrived home from work. Occasionally, he would be out in the garage puttering at some odd job. The house never seemed empty then. There was nothing lonely or too big about the house when he was alive, even if he wasn't in it.

I often felt like my loneliness would overcome me. Yet, I knew there was no choice. I was on a merry-go-round of life. I had to keep going because there was no way to jump off the world. I couldn't get rid of the reality of grief. I'm not sure exactly what kept me going. Maybe it was my human drive, or my desire to live.

Work provided me with daily busyness and that, in some ways, was a godsend. I was able to block out my grief much of the time when I focused on the constant activity of my job. In the midst of it, though, my temporary wall against grief would come crashing down, often when least expected. I could manage to be involved with the tasks and responsibilities of the job and forget for a brief period that Gary was gone. For that short respite from grief, life appeared normal. Then the overwhelming thought would smack against me again: "Oh, my gosh, he has died."

This return to reality bowled me over like a sudden wave on a stormy sea. These deep feelings of emptiness knocked the air out of me. I was shocked at how powerful those feelings of grief were. I had no idea of their intensity, even though I had studied grief, spoken about it, and journeyed with others in their bereavement. Gary's death taught me that there is no way we can fully perceive what the experience of grief is like without our own significant loss.

Gary never went to the grocery store with me, so why was going there difficult for me after he was gone? I guess it was that constant yearning to have him back. Whenever I met up with couples in the grocery store or anywhere else, the feeling arose in me that, if he were just alive, everything would be okay. I wouldn't let myself believe that I was ever angry with him, or that he ever did anything wrong. I knew in my head this wasn't true, but what I knew in my head and what I felt in my heart didn't match anymore. Unconsciously, I avoided remembering anything except the best things about Gary.

In my loneliness, I didn't feel like a complete person. I didn't know who I was. I'd look in the mirror and wonder who it was that looked back at me. I had never been a widow before and that person looking back at me was a stranger. During my time of grieving, I had to put forth every bit of energy to function from day to day. I also had to get to know the new person that I was. I wanted to be strong for my children and for those that I worked with in hospice. All of those people depended on me and I didn't want to disappoint them.

I gradually learned to be with the pain and not try to run from it, but it was so difficult. The pain hurt deeply. None of my children lived in Des Moines, but they were great about coming home. My son Mike lived in Atlanta and came to visit about every six weeks. Considering the great distance, his trips were a real sacrifice. I looked forward to his coming home. He called almost every day. I knew he was grieving, too. My daughter Julie came home every time she had two days off together, which was once or twice a month. She also called me every day. I told both Julie and Mike, "You don't have to call so often. I'm okay." Julie said to me one day, "Mom, my phone calls aren't just for you. I need them as much as you do."

My son Joe called as often as he could, but he was finishing medical school and was dealing with the pressures of that world. My children had their own journeys of grief and there we all were, trying to be strong for each other. When Julie or Mike left after the weekend to go back to their homes, I felt desperate for them to stay, but I tried to be brave, knowing they were hurting too. I waited until they were out of sight; then I went back into the house and sobbed my heart out.

I also noticed that my children were concerned about my health. They kept asking me if I'd had a recent medical examination. I did seem to have the flu every few months after Gary died. This was unusual because normally I was seldom ill. Julie remarked once, "Mom, you're sick so much. I don't ever remember you being sick when we were growing up." I'm sure my immune system was suffering from my emotional state. (Since then, I've learned that the surviving spouse may often become ill.)

I also discovered that when one parent dies, the children may become increasingly concerned about the other parent. My children expressed this through their constant concern about my health and well-being. This was one of the reasons I was determined not to cave in from my grief. I wanted to ease their worries. My children were a great blessing to me. My love for them motivated me to try to adjust to living alone in a healthy way. I wanted to be there for them in the same way that they were there for me. Gary had gone Home, and we all had to discover how to help each other through our grief.

Meditation

Step out of your activity for a bit and sit down in one of your favorite chairs. Picture yourself alone on a ship at sea. The waves are wild, dipping the boat up and down in stormy waters.

As you are tossed back and forth, the person you are grieving comes and sits beside you. He (she) holds you and encourages you to be at peace.

Gradually the waves cease their wild movement and the water grows amazingly calm. After sitting awhile with you, your loved one tenderly bids you farewell and disappears.

You stay in the boat. The ocean remains serene and gently rocks you like an infant in a cradle.

Prayer

O Divine Peace,
grief washes over me like waves of the sea.
Just when I think I can live with my loss,
I'm suddenly pitched into deep anguish again.
My body and spirit both carry this heartache.
It constantly tumbles and turns inside of me.
Lead me to a balance between quiet and activity
so I can tend my grief but not be overcome by it.
Be with me as an assuring presence in my boat of life
when I am tossed around wildly by this sea of grief.

For Today

I will accept the unpredictable flow of my
emotions, trusting that my grief will eventually cease and the rhythm of my days will be
more peaceful.

CHAPTER FIVE

All Your

Possessions

Are Precious

People give lots of advice about what we should do after our loved one dies, like suggesting when to let go of personal possessions, such as clothes. I've noticed that quite a few of these people with their "good advice" have not had a spouse or someone close to them die. People presume they know what is best for someone else who has said goodbye. Some well-meaning persons will counsel, "You need to get rid of his clothes now. It's

been long enough." No one except the one who is grieving should decide when the time is right to let go of a
loved one's possessions.

All of those things that I never thought about
before Gary's death took on great meaning for me
after he was gone. He kept a little book in his front
shirt pocket with a list of the things he was going to do
each day. He would cross the items off the list as he
completed them. I used to get a little irritated waiting
for him to cross certain things off that list of his, like
home repair projects. Now I treasure those miniature
calendar books. They are like entering his personal
diary. Gary made notes: "Get Joyce a birthday card, an
anniversary card," or "Julie, Joe, and Mike are coming
home." Every happening important to Gary was pen-
ciled on those pages. These precious books go back
several years, which allows me to see what he did and
when he did it. The lists give me a good sense of what
was on his mind each day.

Every thing, however small, took on significance
after his death, even though it did not mean anything
in particular when Gary was alive. Shirts I never paid
much attention to brought back memories of when I
purchased them or where he went when he wore
them. Going through his chest of drawers, the children and I found birthday cards and valentines we
gave him that he had saved. We didn't know they
meant that much to him. Seeing those mementoes, I

felt I never wanted to throw away anything that he valued.

Gary went Home to God in June and that autumn I decided I would give his winter coats, boots, thick socks, and other cold-weather items to the homeless, so that his clothing could keep them warm. This motivation helped me to get his clothes boxed up. I felt that these things would serve a purpose and this decision would have pleased him.

Surprisingly, Gary's shaving kit was one of the most difficult things to discard. I kept it in the bathroom drawer for more than two years because it seemed to belong there. That kit became a precious reminder of the one I loved. It gave me a warm feeling whenever I saw it and assured me that a little part of him was still with me.

Another difficult thing to let go of was our camper. When Gary was alive, we spent many weekends camping. Selling that possession, with all the memories attached to it, was especially painful, but I knew I would never use it again by myself and the kids weren't interested in it at the time. The day that the new owner came, paid for the camper, and drove out of the driveway with it, I felt like a rock was being sucked out of my chest. Nausea overtook me as he pulled the camper down the street. Seeing it being taken away made Gary's death so final. He loved camping, and through the years had taught me to enjoy it too. With the camper gone, a large piece of who Gary was went down the street and out of sight.

My husband's incredible garage was his shrine. He had every tool imaginable; some he made himself. Everything was well organized, labeled, and displayed in a way that showed his tools to be his most priceless possessions. I never thought much about his shop until after he died. Then I would go out there and marvel at how neat and creative Gary was. My son Mike offered to help me sort the collection of tools so I could begin to part with them. We gave some to his friends; the rest Mike was able to use because he was a woodworker and craftsman like his dad. Of course, these tools took on a new significance to Mike because they belonged to his dad.

There were some things I was happy to give away. Gary had been a packrat and it was a joy to get rid of twenty-five years' worth of old magazines and boxes filled to the brim with all sorts of stuff. My children and I had many laughs about some of the things he chose to save.

As I continued to grieve, I noticed that we let go of Gary's possessions a little at a time, when we thought it was the best moment to do so. I don't think there is any right or wrong time to divest of what a loved one leaves behind. It depends on each grieving person. As we face parting with these items, it is another small way to start healing from our loss.

Those whom we loved dearly would have no idea how much we value their belongings. As we go through their possessions and eventually part with them, it helps us to grieve. We become willing to let go of the material things that are dear to us because we know we will always have the storehouse of memories those mementoes brought to us.

Meditation

Select a small item that was once a part of your loved one's life.

Touch it. Smell it. Place this item on your lap or set it in front of you. Fix your gaze upon this item. Allow memories of your loved one to arise.

Close your eyes and visualize these memories being placed in a golden treasure box. Speak to God about these treasures.

Listen to how God responds to you.

Prayer

Bountiful Giver of Love,
the material things of _____ pull me into grief.
These simple items have become significant to me.
As I face the finality of letting these mementoes go,

assure me that my love is vaster and more enduring
than any physical thing my loved one used or wore.
The treasure of our love will always be in my heart.
I have a storehouse of memories to keep that love alive.
When it is time to divest myself of these possessions,
with your strength and encouragement, help me to do so.

For Today

I will put away (or give away) one of my loved one's possessions.

CHAPTER SIX

Others Just Don't

Understand

After Gary's death, friends and family members continued to call to see how I was doing. Everyone tried to be caring and thoughtful. My phone rang frequently from Monday until Friday. Then, no one called from Friday until Monday. It quickly became obvious that everyone was busy with their own lives during the weekend.

What they did not realize is that weekends, especially Sundays, are some of the loneliest and quietest for those who are widowed. When I went to the shopping mall to walk and be around people, all I saw were couples. I told my daughter one Sunday when she

called that "only couples were walking at the mall."
She responded, "Mom, there are no more couples than
there ever were in the mall. It's just that this is all you
notice." She was right. When your spouse dies, it does
seem like all the world is made up of couples.

Another frustration that I experienced is quite
common to most people who grieve. When friends
called to ask how I was doing, I often mentioned my
husband in the conversation. When I did this, they
quickly changed the subject. I soon discovered that no
one wanted to talk about him. They did not understand that he was, and is, my favorite subject. When I
started talking about him, I sensed their reluctance to
carry on the conversation. They tried to avoid the subject, thinking it would only make me sad. But I was,
and am, actually filled with warmth and gratitude
when anyone speaks about my husband or when I am
able to share memories of him.

When Gary was alive, we belonged to a group of
twelve couples who attended the playhouse six times
a year. After the play we went to each other's homes
for snacks and beverages. The first time I tried to go to
the playhouse by myself after Gary died, the seat next
to me was empty. This was his reserved seat and the
place he would have filled. That night the space gaped
as wide and empty as the one in my heart. One-third
of the way through the play I excused myself, got up,
and went home. I couldn't bear the devastating reality
of Gary's absence. None of the couples I was with gave

that empty seat a second thought, because each of them still had a spouse filling the seat next to them.

Not one of the friends I went to the playhouse with that night called the next day to see why I had left so abruptly. They were all caring people, but they obviously didn't realize what attending the play without Gary could possibly have been like for me. During the following year, at the party after a play, I would often bring up Gary's name because I wanted something of him to still be a part of the group. Whenever I spoke about him, though, I felt the uneasiness of those present. This discomfort increased my sadness. It seemed like no one except me missed him enough to talk about him. This created even more distress. I asked myself, "How could they have forgotten him so quickly?"

A few years after Gary's death, a woman in our playhouse group died of cancer. Her husband came to my house about eight or nine months after that and asked to talk with me. He told me that since his wife's death he thought a lot about how I must have felt in the months after Gary died. He realized that our mutual friends had not been supportive of me. It was only after he was spouseless that he became aware of what I went through. He explained, "I didn't want to talk about Gary because he was such a good friend. I missed him greatly and I didn't want to feel the full extent of that loss. I thought this was true for you, too."

My friend's comments helped me understand that there is no way to truly know what grief is like until one has experienced it personally. The friends in our couples group were grieving Gary's loss but they thought they were helping me by not mentioning him. They believed it would increase my sadness. Little did they know how much it could have comforted me. I felt that same way myself before I lost someone I dearly loved.

In my widows bereavement group, we knew, without having to describe in detail, what each one was experiencing. When we were together we would talk and talk about our spouses and know that each one there understood our need to do so. It was comforting to be with people on the same journey. Even though we were each approaching our losses a bit differently, we found many common threads in our experience.

I remember going to dinner one evening with two women whom I had known years earlier, but hadn't seen for a long time. One of the women worked at the same institution where Gary had been. She proceeded to tell me about many of her conversations with Gary. She described how he talked to her about me, how much he loved and appreciated me, and what a good relationship he felt we had.

That was one of the most wonderful evenings, if not *the* most wonderful, that I had had since he died. I could have listened to her all evening. In fact, I found myself tempted to ask her to repeat what he had said.

I felt like a child, but it meant so much to hear about his talks with her. It was like having a little piece of Gary back again.

I hope I do not forget the importance of talking to others about the significant person in their life who has died. I want to remember that this person is their favorite subject.

Meditation

Pause to spend a few moments with your grieving process. Clothe yourself in the Holy One's compassion. Whisper your loved one's name. Savor that name and all that this name means to you.

Bring forth a special remembrance of this person. Find as much comfort as you can in this memory of him (her).

Imagine what your loved one would want to say to you as you experience your journey of grief. Be at peace.

Prayer

Dear God,

how is it that so few people really understand my grief?

Why is it that others fear to talk to me about _____?

Don't they know how comforting it is to hear a story or a name?

If only they realized their comments relieve my grieving spirit

and ease my sadness like a soft raindrop on a drooping flower.

These spoken thoughts help me keep my memories alive.

They assure me that _____ will not be forgotten.

Help me overlook the unawareness or insensitivity of others

and their inability to know how little it takes to comfort me.

For Today

I will say my loved one's name aloud or quietly in my heart whenever I am feeling lonely
or sad.

CHAPTER SEVEN

Those Dreaded

First Holidays

When someone significant to us dies, the holidays take on a different shape without that person. The widow's group I belonged to formed about two years after Gary died. There were only a few of us in the beginning, but it quickly grew in size. We named our group SSENIPPAH, which is "Happiness" spelled backward. We thought that name was significant because the death of our spouses definitely turned our lives around backward.

Every Wednesday evening we met for dinner either at a restaurant or at someone's home. We took time at each gathering to share the particular struggle of that week, or what we especially missed about our husbands. Our first gathering was on Valentine's Day. While not an official holiday, we felt this day was particularly difficult, even if we didn't do anything special to commemorate it when our husbands were alive. Some of the women spoke about how alone they felt on this day that is dedicated to love. Some regretted not making more of Valentine's Day when their husbands were alive. Now they would never have a chance to celebrate it with them.

SSENIPPAH is still an active group and has been meeting for more than twelve years. While it varies in size, there are usually thirty to forty members. These women feel it is a special blessing to be able to share the journey of widowhood together because the members of the group offer a lot of support to one another. Valentine's Day and New Year's Eve are two of the holidays on which SSENIPPAH makes sure to have a gathering so the widows will be with someone on these two occasions that most couples celebrate.

Before Gary's death and before our widow's group started meeting, I heard grieving people remark about how difficult Christmas, birthdays, or anniversaries were. I thought I knew what they were talking about. However, I realized after living those months without my husband that I didn't understand at all what their experiences were like. After Gary died, the holidays took on a feeling of dread instead of the familiar one of excitement and anticipation.

The Fourth of July was always a special holiday for our family. Ever since the kids were little, we had held a picnic in our backyard. It quickly became a tradition. We fixed burgers. Everyone who came brought a food dish of some sort. The kids had sparklers and we all had great fun. After the kids grew up, the same people continued coming to our house for the picnic. The first Fourth of July after Gary died was excruciating. All those wonderful memories brought so much sadness.

I dreaded the thought of going through the first Christmas without Gary. As this anxiety grew in me, I proceeded to do something several months prior to Christmas that proved to be extremely helpful in softening my grief. For their Christmas gift, I decided to make the kids a photo album of each of their lives with their dad. I went through boxes and boxes of photos looking for the best ones. Some snapshots I had reprinted if I wanted to put the same one in each of their books. Putting those photo albums together was bittersweet. Some nights I fell into a well of sadness as I sat and looked at photos from our wedding and other special events. At other times, I experienced pure joy when I came across pictures I had forgotten.

Each of the three books were divided into four sections: birth to kindergarten, first grade to high school, high school through college, and college until present. Those pictures of the kids and their dad were more rewarding than I could ever have imagined. I wrote significant comments under the photos to jumpstart their memories, or to explain what they were too little to remember.

I started each book with our wedding picture, and on the last page of the book was a large picture of the double rainbow in the sky the night their dad died. We saw the rainbow when we came out of the hospital that night. It was a powerful moment for us because Gary loved nature, especially rainbows. We decided that he was waving goodbye to us.

The kids loved their Christmas gifts. The photo albums were also a gift to me because making them provided me with considerable consolation. I recommend creating photo albums as a tool to assist with grieving.

That year I wasn't going to put up a tree because I didn't think I could stand to do it. The night before Christmas Eve, I was sitting in Gary's chair and it hit me how selfish I was being. I thought, "Just because you're too depressed to decorate a tree, you're going to deprive the kids of coming home to a festive house." It occurred to me that this holiday wasn't just about me; they were grieving too. Not having a Christmas tree would only add to their loss. That thought was the motivation I needed to move out of my chair and get the tree up. I spent the entire evening and into the early morning decorating it. I even kind of enjoyed the process. When I finished, the house seemed less lonely. It felt more normal and I knew I had done the right thing.

When the kids came home on Christmas Eve, they seemed relieved. Things looked fairly typical with the tree being there. We had made plans to fly a day later to my oldest son's house in New York. We wanted to all be together and decided going there would be something different than we had done before. We hoped it would be good for us. We were clearly all trying hard to be as happy as we could be, even though the void created by Gary's absence was obvious.

We spent three days at Joe and Annmarie's in New York and even went skiing in Vermont one day. It was about as nice a Christmas as it could be, given our loss. But I was surprised at how lonely I felt even in the midst of my family. I asked myself, "How can I feel so incredibly alone when I am with my children, whom I love with all my heart?" Even though I tried to get rid of it, a deep ache the size of an enormous boulder lodged inside of me. Their dad was missing from our celebration and it was impossible to get around this fact. I knew that no matter what we did for the holiday, that ache was going to remain.

As I went through the first year's celebrations, there was simply no way I could avoid the consequences of what the loss of Gary did to my attempt to join in events meant to be happy occasions. Only by the grace and strength of God did I manage to make it through those celebrations without falling further into my loneliness.

Meditation

Sit down with paper and pen in hand. Close your eyes and remember you are not alone. God has infinite compassion for you and is a steady presence of constant care. Welcome this love into your heart.

Open your eyes and write the name of the day being commemorated (holiday, birthday, anniversary). Jot down your memories of past celebrations in words, phrases, or sentences.

When you complete the list, open your hands, palms up, and place them under the paper. Hold the list out with gratitude for what has been, and with trust that you have the strength you need to make it through what lies ahead.

Then set the paper aside as a sign of your willingness to let go and to be open to what will be.

Prayer

God of compassion,
how can I enter into the celebration of this day
when my heart is far removed from festivity?
How can I be a part of what is meant to be joyful?

All I can think of is _____, who is missing.
There is no easy plan to lift grief from these occasions.
I simply have to make it through the day as best I can.
As I do so, I remember the assurance of your presence
and the strength that comes through those who care.
Keep my focus on what can lessen and ease my sorrow.

For Today

I will be gentle with myself and be grateful
for what has been.

CHAPTER EIGHT

Grandma,

but No Grandpa

More couples today are enjoying the gift of growing old together. I am continually amazed at my neighbors who are in their eighties and enjoying sixty-plus years of marriage. They tell me stories about their grandchildren being parents and how they delight in watching their great-grandchildren grow.

I often wonder what it would have been like if Gary had lived to see all three of his children marry. What would he have been like as a grandpa? No doubt, he might have gotten a little overwhelmed with the commotion those little ones create, as he did occasionally with his own three children when they were young. Joe and Mike were not quite a year apart and there were often two or three more of their friends in the house, so the racket got to him sometimes. One of the central reasons for his being bothered by the noisy house of three children was his cancer. The children were two, four, and five years of age when he was diagnosed. Not feeling well made any kind of tumult intolerable at times.

Gary wasn't used to lots of activity in a home because he grew up in a household of only his parents and himself. His brother was fifteen years older than him and was married when Gary was four years old. So his family's house was quiet most of the time. Gary's parents were in their forties when he was born and always seemed kind of old to him. They wanted the house quiet in the evening when all three of them were there together.

So I wonder what he would have been like as a grandfather. I picture him playing with the grandkids and I know he would have been proud of them. There are certain things about each of their personalities that I think he would have enjoyed. He often told me he hoped he would live long enough so we could be "Grandpa and Grandma" and grow old together.

When my first grandchild, Emma, was born, I drove to Kansas City and arrived there just before my daughter gave birth. All the way there I experienced a quiet sorrow because I had to make the trip alone. This was not how it was supposed to be. When I first saw little Emma, I again experienced that terrible aching in my chest. Such an acute emptiness. I felt like a big hole was there where "Grandpa Gary" was meant to be. The loneliness I felt in the midst of the joy of my first grandchild took away some of the thrill of being "Grandma" for the first time. "Why did it have to be this way?" I kept thinking. Yet, I set aside my sadness because it was such a happy time for Julie and Mike. I didn't want to take away from that moment in any way.

My daughter Julie insists that the reason why all of my grandchildren are beautiful is because "Dad walked around heaven and picked out each one of them." Julie smiles as she goes on, "I picture him saying, 'I will take that one for Joe, and that one for Mike, and that one for Julie.'" Those kinds of thoughts console and help us as we try to make sense of the loss we still feel. Most of all, those consolations help us to trust that Gary is a part of our life with the grandchildren, even though he is not physically present with us.

My family was concerned that the grandchildren would never know their grandpa. My daughter-in-law Carter described how she remembers her grandfather although she never got to meet him in person. She was told so many stories and wonderful things about her grandfather that he became bigger than life to her. Carter ended with, "He never could have measured up to the grandpa I imagined from the descriptions I listened to since I was a small girl." Carter's comment helped us because my family has told my nine grand-children so many stories about their Grandpa Gary that there's little doubt he, too, has also become larger than life to them. So, even though they never got to know their grandfather when he was alive, the grand-children talk about him as if they know him well.

Gary, even though we didn't get to grow old together and be Grandpa and Grandma together, your grandchil-dren will know you well. The goal of my journey without you now is to help them to know who you are. And, by the way, thanks for picking out such beautiful grandchildren to send to our family.

Meditation

Gather photos of your spouse and your grand-children or great grandchildren. Place these before you or hold them in your lap.

Recall the esteemed values and revered qualities of the deceased grandparent that you wish he (she) could have shared with the grandchildren.

Look at the photos of the grandchildren. Visualize this grandparent blessing them. As he (she) embraces each grandchild, imagine each of them being filled with the goodness of their deceased grandparent's spirit.

Then close your eyes and choose one happy memory of times past with this grandparent. Let it warm your heart with love.

Prayer

Gracious One,
thank you for the gift of my grandchildren.
When I grow sad with remembering
that _____ is missing from their lives,
remind me to tell them stories about him (her).
Help me keep that beautiful memory alive
and to pass _____'s goodness on to them.
Most of all, I entrust my dear grandchildren
into the vigilant presence of your loving care.
Watch over them and guide them on their way.

For Today

I will entrust my grandchildren into God's
care and be grateful for the gift they are in
my life.

CHAPTER NINE

I'm the

Only One Left

When my youngest brother Gene died, he was the last of my family of origin. Both my parents were deceased, as well as my other three brothers. I couldn't believe that, of our family of seven, I was the only one left. With Gene gone, I felt an awful loneliness. Soon after he died, though, busyness took over my life and I unconsciously set aside my sadness over his death. Six weeks later, I went to the funeral of my husband's uncle. I didn't know this man, so I was stunned when a powerful flow of tears engulfed me during the funeral service. All through the eulogy and singing, each of my family members who had died kept coming to mind. As I look back on that moment, it was almost like I was attending the funeral of my entire family at the same time.

When I came home that night, I experienced a heartbreaking desire to be with my family. While I was preparing dinner, I pictured my mom walking up to the deck of our house. In my longing for her, I realized I was as homesick for her and the rest of my family as I was for Gene. That evening my heart felt like it was going to break. There was an indescribable hurt in the middle of my chest. Oh, how I wished I could see, talk to, hear, or do whatever I could to connect once more with those dear people. Tears kept flowing and I could not stop them from coming.

The more I thought of my family, the more I yearned to sit with them for a while. "If only I could do this," I thought, "then I will be okay." Even while I was thinking this, I realized my desire came out of the eruption of grief that was hidden in the corner of my heart. I had not given enough time to my grief over Gene's death. Now it was calling out for attention. This surge of loss eventually lessened, but there were still days and weeks after that when the longing to be with my deceased family rose up strongly in me.

When this accumulated grief for my family members cried out for attention, I took time to write in my journal. Here is one of my entries:

To think that I won't see any of them again until I die is just devastating. I do believe they are happy, but I feel such an aching loneliness for them. When I think about my family history and traditions, I feel like an orphan, like they forgot about me and left me behind. I have my children, my new husband and his family, and I am grateful for all of them, but no one can replace the family that I grew up with. I think about holidays, summers, my childhood school days, the many significant people. Now, all of that is gone—forever.

After I tended to this intense episode of grief, I continued to have fleeting thoughts of wondering if my family members missed me. In the middle of something I was doing, my mind would flood with images of Mom, Dad, and my four brothers. I could picture them clearly, just as they used to be when we gathered together.

Sometimes I longed for one person more than another, but most of the time I missed all six of them at once. Whenever I hear people refer to their brothers or sisters, their remarks often lead me to a memory of some activity or enjoyable situation that involved one or more of my brothers and myself. Occasionally, I still find myself puzzled by the reality that they have all died and I am still here. I'm glad to be alive, but it feels strange to be the only one left.

I have learned from past painful times that if I befriend grief and allow myself to cry as much as I need, the pain will eventually pass. If I try to swallow the hurt or hold it inside myself, I have difficulty breathing and the world around me fills with a dark sense of hopelessness. I'm grateful that my loneliness for my family did not stay hidden inside me and that I was able to tend to the sorrow that visited me.

One of the best helps in mourning the death of a loved one is to stay with my grief and to give myself permission to feel those emotions as much as I can. It is the only way I can survive the loss of someone dear. As I allow my grief to come forth, I tell myself, "My heart is broken today, but there will come a time when this heartache no longer sweeps over me and consumes me."

As I continue to allow grief to come forth, I try to remember that I hurt this way because of the vast love I have for my family. How blessed I am to have had them to enjoy and love. I hope when I go Home they will be waiting with open arms for me to join them.

Meditation

Choose a room that has some open space. Walk around the room in a circle, slowly, deliberately.

As you walk, name the people you cherish who have gone Home before you.

Imagine that each one is there in the circle with you. Welcome their presence and receive their love. Continue walking in the circle until you have taken time with each one of them and have been blessed by the memory of their presence.

Prayer

All-embracing One,
loneliness threatens to take over my life.
It unravels the fibers of my concentration
and impedes my peace of mind and heart.
Not a day or night goes by without longing
for the companionship and love of _____.
When this strong part of grief grabs hold of me,
help me hear what lies beneath my loneliness:
the depth of love that binds me to _____.
Let me be gentle with the heartache that I feel.

For Today

I will embrace the goodness that each
deceased person brought into my life and try
to share this goodness with others.

CHAPTER TEN

I Lost a Part

of Myself

I was born twenty minutes before my twin brother Joe. It was our mother's birthday. Joe and I slept together in the same baby bed because our parents couldn't afford separate ones. We shared everything about our lives as we grew up. Mom used to say, "Those two have a language nobody else understands." Even though we had two older brothers we were often unaware of them. Joe and I were like each other's shadows.

From the time we were small, I assigned myself the job of taking care of my twin. We were four years old when we went to stay with Aunt Lenore while

Mom gave birth to our younger brother, Gene. When we returned home, Aunt Lenore informed our mother: "I changed things when the twins were with me. I wouldn't let Joyce dress Joe or put on his shoes. I made him do things for himself." This became a joke in the family, but that comment really did reflect my mothering of Joe.

When the two of us were in school, I'd be concerned if Joe talked when he shouldn't, or if he was being punished. I also liked to help him with his homework. He probably got tired of my constant attention although he never indicated it. In high school we weren't in the same classes all the time, and I was glad. I tended to worry about Joe because he was much more of a daredevil than I was and easily got in trouble. We enjoyed sharing friends, which was convenient in many ways. Our classmates loved it when we had parties because he invited his boy friends and I invited my girl friends.

As graduation drew near, Joe became increasingly rebellious toward my parents. They were strict and punished him severely, sometimes with whippings. Joe and I differed in this area because I followed the rules while he continually defied them. He also started drinking beer with the boys and had some "run-ins" with the law. Mom cried about his behavior and insisted she was going crazy with worry. Dad increased the physical punishment. I felt burdened with my mother's sadness and anxious about Joe. During our senior year, I'd often wait up for him to come home in order to sneak him into the house without our parents knowing he was late, hoping to prevent Dad's punishment and Mom's distress.

Graduation came and the two of us walked in side by side for the ceremony. That was a special moment but we both were a little frightened, wondering how we would deal with being separated when we went our own ways. I planned to go to nursing school in Iowa and Joe was going with his friend Bob to Oklahoma to work on the wheat harvest.

We weathered that first summer apart but were lonesome for each other. We talked on the phone as much as we could, but that wasn't easy in 1958. I remember Joe calling from Oklahoma one evening when I was in the nursing school dorm. He told me he didn't miss home but he missed me a lot. We talked for quite a while that night and reminded each other that we would always stay close no matter how many miles separated us. I was surprised by our conversation. I didn't know Joe felt so deeply about me, even though I always knew we were closely connected.

Time passed. Joe worked on construction in Missouri. I graduated from nursing school and worked at Mercy Hospital. I dated and fell in love with Gary. I wanted Joe to know Gary and to give me feedback about him. Joe and I always gave our opinions about who we were dating. If Joe didn't think the person I was going with in high school was good for me, he'd tell me so. I did the same for him. Fortunately, Gary was from our hometown so Joe knew him and readily approved of our plans to be engaged.

When Gary and I married, Joe was our best man and seemed happy at the wedding. After we returned from our honeymoon a week later, Mom commented, "I'm so glad you're home. Joe has been a crabby bear the whole time you've been gone. I think he's a little mad that you got married." Later that evening when Joe and I were alone, I asked him if he was upset about my marriage. He hesitated for quite a while and then responded, "I guess so, kinda." I assured him that no one would ever take his place and invited him to come to Des Moines to spend the next weekend with us. Joe stayed with us two nights and the three of us had a great time. While I worked at the hospital during the day, he and Gary hung out together. Joe spent several weekends with us that way and quickly realized that our relationship had not changed.

Three months later, I woke up out of a sound sleep at about 4:30 on a Tuesday morning and felt something was terribly wrong with my twin brother. I paced the floor and thought, "I can't call anyone at this hour." After some time in prayer, I decided to go to the 6:00 a.m. Mass at the hospital before work.

When I came out of Mass forty-five minutes later, a friend's parents, who lived in Des Moines, were standing in the hallway waiting for me. They said they had bad news. I asked them if something had happened to

Joe. They nodded and told me Joe had been killed in a car accident on his way to Leon. He had fallen asleep at the wheel, gone into the ditch, and hit a tree.

I couldn't believe it, even though in the pit of my stomach I had known something dreadful like that had happened. I found out later that the accident occurred at the very time I woke up.

I had only been married a few months and there I was, trying to cope with the death of the most significant person in my life. I couldn't let myself think about it for fear I'd fall apart. I tried to put it out of my mind as best I could.

Strange things happened to me, though. All of a sudden I was afraid of the dark. I couldn't sleep. When I finally did get to sleep, I had terrible dreams about things happening to people I loved.

I tried to be busy and not think about Joe. It didn't seem fair to Gary, being newly married, for me to be sad, so I just refused to let myself think about Joe's death. I was aware of an empty place in the middle of my chest, but I didn't talk to anyone about it. I was sure that if I stayed busy I could deal with it and never think about my pain or the loss of Joe again.

The one thing I was aware of was that I felt a bit like mercury—like I was not going to be able to contain myself in my skin. It was like my left arm needed to be attached to something or it would just run in all directions. It finally occurred to me one day that my skin was starving to connect with Joe. The two of us had slept together in the same womb and as infants and as toddlers in one bed. The skin I had been attached to was gone forever. Once I knew why I was feeling this way, my skin hunger gradually ended.

Joe, I can't wait to see you in heaven. You loved me more unconditionally than I could ever expect. We were truly one. In fact, it was sometimes hard to determine where you stopped and I started. I learned from your death that we can't just ignore grief. It waits for us and won't go away until we pay attention to it. I grieved your death twenty-two years later when Mom died. It felt then as if you had just died. My heart ached for you and I finally cried those many tears that I held back at the time of your death. I guess ignoring death doesn't work, does it?

Meditation

Picture yourself in a comforting, nurturing space that is shaped like a womb. Inside this safe place love abounds. The atmosphere is one of total relaxation and complete serenity. Each time you breathe in, your grieving self absorbs tenderness.

As you rest in this consolation, you discover you are not alone. Someone is with you in this tender space. This is the person you were intimately bonded with when he (she) was alive.

The two of you draw near to one another and rest in the treasured love that blessed your relationship. Be at peace.

Prayer

Dear Womb of Love,
no matter how difficult life is for me,
you are always there to uphold me in love.
I turn to you now for reassurance and comfort
as I grieve the death of _____.
Carry me in the womb of your compassion.
Heal that part of myself that seems to have left.
When my mind and heart wander about in sadness,
draw me close to your nurturing presence.
Help the endless ache in my heart to heal.

For Today

Each time grief rises up and presses against
my heart, I will remember that I am held in
the womb of God's compassion.

STORIES

OF GRIEF

BY OTHERS

CHAPTER ELEVEN

You Weren't There

for My Wedding

BY JULIE L.

"I just want to live long enough to walk Julie down the aisle." I heard these words dozens of times growing up. My dad began saying this after he was given a prognosis of six months to live. I was two-and-a-half at the time. It was more than duty that led my dad to want to be there for my wedding; I was the only girl with two older brothers, and our father-daughter bond developed early.

The years my dad was home battling his terminal cancer were truly a gift for the two of us. The diagnosis of lymphoma and its grim prognosis sent my mother to work to support our family and left Dad at home. At first Mom was not able to leave me at home with him, but as he grew stronger (and I grew a little older) we spent our days together. I "worked" beside him as he puttered in the garage with his woodworking, baked imaginary cakes for him in the dishwasher, and played beauty shop with him as my client. (He was very tolerant of the bows I tied in his hair and beard.) Even though he was ill, I never thought of him as anything other than my dad—just like everyone else's. Looking back I'm sure he was much more attentive and present to me than most fathers who were working stressful jobs. This is what made his illness a gift to me.

We continued our close relationship as I grew up. Dad was patient with the teenage angst of my brothers and myself. I remember many times hearing him give Mom a pep talk when she was discouraged about how much time we spent with friends or when my brother seemed unmanageable. I always knew when I came in late, either from work or from hanging out with friends, that Dad would still be sitting up watching television. I loved to sit down on the other end of the sofa and watch with him, or chat about my night. I get my night-owl blood from him.

After I graduated from college and moved to another city, I came home at least twice a month, sometimes for three or four days at a time, depending on how my days off landed. I was a hospital staff nurse and worked three twelve-hour shifts each week. I really enjoyed hanging out with my parents and still had a lot of good friends at home. On one visit I ran into a friend I hadn't seen in a while. Mike was going to be in the town where I lived and I told him to call me. I found out later that he made up a reason to come so we could spend time together without the distraction of other friends.

After we began dating, I took Mike home to meet my parents. Dad immediately liked him and was excited to see this chapter of my life unfold. When Mike and I decided to get married, I knew my dad was pleased—not just for the prospect of getting to take that walk down the aisle but because he truly thought Mike was a great guy and would make a wonderful husband for his precious girl.

After we set a date for November of that year and started preparing for the wedding, Dad began having issues with abdominal pain. Eventually it was determined that he needed to have a second heart bypass surgery. The night before he was to go in for surgery my mom and I went to the florist to order the wedding flowers. I will never forget coming home to see my dad sitting outside in a patio chair. I sat down with him and he asked me how it went with the florist. After hearing the details, he said, "I just want you to know how much I am looking forward to this wedding." I replied, "Me too, Dad."

My father did not survive that surgery. In the following days of planning the funeral, the last thing I wanted to think about was "a stupid wedding" or even getting married at all. I knew I was pushing Mike away but I just couldn't see how he could fit into my life then. The night of the wake service my mom called me into her room to talk. She had lost her brother soon after she and my dad were married, so she was able to speak from the heart. I will never forget her telling me: "It's hard to love with a broken heart but your dad would never want you to give up your marriage." Those words saved my future.

When Mom and I went to the credit union to close Dad's account, we discovered he had created a fund for my wedding dress. There was a note attached to Dad's account that read, "This account is to purchase my daughter's wedding dress, the last 'Raggedy Ann' dress that I will buy for her."

When I was about seven years old, the two of us went shopping. It was my birthday and Dad wanted us to have some special time together. He bought me a red Raggedy Ann dress that day. It was long and fancy, hanging almost to the floor. I loved it, even though Mom didn't think it was "very practical."

We were both shocked that Dad had kept this desire of his a secret. The discovery was sad and beautiful at the same time. It was as if Dad knew he would not be there for the wedding.

When people found out I was engaged, it was followed with excited congratulations and inquiries about the wedding details. I would always start with a "But my dad just died . . ." I felt like this was such a part of who I was, not just a bride-to-be but a broken-hearted bride-to-be with no dad to walk her down the aisle.

I made it through the wedding day, but much of it was a blur. My mom walked me down the aisle. I sobbed my heart out the entire way. It all felt like much more of an obligation than anything else. I wanted to be married but felt the day was almost more a day of sadness than of joy. I look back at the pictures and can see the sadness through my smiles.

It has now been fourteen years, and those two events—my dad's death and my wedding—seem to be one and the same. It took me a long time to realize that every year on my wedding anniversary a part of me relives the grief and sadness. Each year I am reminded of the day that my father and I waited so long for and didn't get to share.

I was telling someone about this recently and she suggested that maybe someday Mike and I should renew our vows and have a little gathering to make the date the joyous occasion that it should be. At the time I thought it was a good idea, but later I realized that the connection is not something I want to give up. The sadness I feel on this day reminds me of the two most wonderful men in my life and how they both love me so much. I can't change the way things happened, so I don't want to change the memories. I celebrate on this day that Mike and I have had another year together and look forward to many more. But I will always carry with me that little bit of heartache that is part of who I am. I'm afraid if I ever gave that up I might forget the man that I loved so dearly for the first twenty-seven years of my life.

Meditation

Visualize a future anticipated event of success and joy. Your father (mother) will not be there. What part of this absence causes you the greatest sadness?

Again visualize this significant event. Open your heart to the joy and blessing that this experience can hold for you.

Call to mind the face of your father (mother). Imagine him (her) giving you a special blessing. What words of wisdom do you hear? Close your eyes and let these words of wisdom find a home in your heart.

Prayer

Divine Companion,
you are with me on this journey.
Your love steadies and strengthens me.
As I experience this special moment
without _____'s being here,
help me to embrace the joy amid my sadness.
Keep turning my heart toward your love
as I struggle with my mixed emotions.
Thank you for the gift of _____,
who went Home to you much too soon.
Turn me toward joy as you walk with me.

For Today

I will let joy and sorrow be present in my
heart while I keep my focus on love.

 My Daughter's

Death

BY SUZIE F.

It was January 2, 1995. For the first time in six months I slept through the night. I woke up to the sound of three happy little boys playing in the family room with their dad. I remember thinking that I hadn't been this relaxed in a long time, and thanking God for my beautiful family. Scott and I had been married six years so far. Aryn, nine, and Bryan, thirteen, came with Scott. Margo, who was six at the time, came with me, and together Scott and I had three sons, fifteen months apart. It was a busy, wonderful household.

Margo had gone with her father and stepmother to Kansas to see her grandparents. Aryn and Bryan were at their mother's. So Scott and I were home with the babies, aged three, two, and six months. I was with everyone in the family room when the phone rang at 8:30 a.m. I remember Scott answering it and handing it to me with concern in his eyes. It was Margo's dad, Brent.

He began by saying that they had been in a car accident. I asked if everyone was okay. He responded, "No—oh, honey, Margo is dead." I threw the phone down and fell to the floor. My knees would no longer support my body. I was aware of a guttural scream and of wailing, "No! No! Not my baby!"

After some time, I returned to the phone and told Brent to stay with her until I was able to get there. This was easier said than done, as Margo had died on an interstate highway by Manhattan, Kansas, which was about a four-hour drive in good weather, and it was snowing heavily at the time. I immediately called my best friend and told her that Margo was dead. Family and friends began arriving soon after to help with the boys.

Scott and I chartered a plane to fly to Kansas. While waiting at the airport, I made calls to Margo's friends and family to let them know what had happened. I remember trying to stay busy so I wouldn't have to think about what I was going to have to face. It was snowy and freezing when we arrived at the

Manhattan airport. The drive from there to the hospital was silent and tense. The walk into the hospital even more so.

Margo was in a private area in the emergency room. I remember people staring at me. I asked everyone to allow me to go in to see her by myself.

She was lying in bed with her head on a pillow and there was a bandage covering the left side of her face. She was wearing a hospital gown. She was beautiful and still looked alive, like she was just sleeping. I began looking over her entire body just like I did when she was a newborn. I tried to hold her, but since she was twelve, this was hard to accomplish. I had to settle for lying beside her. I was singing to her as I did when she was small: "Hush, little baby, don't say a word." I don't know why. It's just what happened.

I was with my daughter for quite some time, but not nearly long enough. A nun came in to tell me that the funeral home was there for Margo. I told her I wasn't ready. This was repeated several times before she said more forcefully, but kindly, that Margo had to go. The gentlemen moved her to a stretcher and as they rolled her out of the room, I again dropped to my knees, unable to stand. Again the words "NO!" kept coming. I turned to them and told them to please take care of my child and not to leave her alone. They were taking Margo to "prepare" her body so that we could fly her back to Iowa with us.

All of the family sat in the waiting room for hours. Everyone was talking about the coconut pie in the cafeteria. I couldn't imagine eating ever again. It was decided that Scott and I would fly back home with her body in the chartered plane. They were unable to get Margo into the plane in a box, so she was placed in a body bag in two seats in a horizontal position. I sat opposite her. It was unbelievable, truly, to have my beautiful daughter in a body bag beside me. It did feel good to be physically close to her, as it was beginning to sink in that being close to her would not always be possible.

We landed in a blizzard. Men from the funeral home were there and for the second time that day I sent my daughter off with complete strangers in dark suits, in a car without me. Unbelievable!

My house was full of people even though it was late at night. I remember thinking I had no energy to parent my boys, but the youngest, Reed, and I still had a dependent relationship because he was nursing. Everyone left and Reed and I retreated to Margo's room to sleep. I put on her pajamas that were in their usual pile by her bed and cozied under her covers. There was a comfort in being surrounded by her things, but there was a huge pit in my stomach. I read her books, looked at pictures, and tried to sleep, but couldn't. Reed finally nodded off and after several hours I did too.

I woke up the next morning with a hungry little baby and initially felt okay until I was jolted into reality with the sudden reminder that I was in Margo's room and she was dead.

There was a blizzard again on the evening of the visitation for Margo. Crowds of people lined up for hours. I felt weak, as I hadn't eaten much since her death three days earlier. The service was touching and Margo looked beautiful. When it was over, I was aware I would never ever see her beautiful face again, or be able to touch her. I asked the priest if I could possibly spend the night with her in the church. He agreed. My good friend Val stayed with me as well. We listened to music, tapes of Margo singing when she was little. We read the cards on all of the flowers and tried to get comfortable on the hard, narrow pews.

I knelt in front of Margo's body for hours and prayed for strength. I wrote a vow to her to try to live my life in a more kind and loving manner. At 6:00 a.m. I became violently ill. I vomited and had the chills. I lay on the cold tile floor in the church bathroom, wondering if they could postpone the funeral for a day if I was too sick to be there. I stayed in the bathroom for a long time before returning to Margo. I knelt quietly as the sun came through the stained-glass window, shining on her beautiful face. I gently tucked her favorite quilt around her and placed her well-worn teddy bear in with her (a tough decision as I wanted to keep it, too).

Father John arrived shortly after this. He asked me to leave as he was going to do the final preparation and didn't want me to be there. It hit me like a ton of bricks that I would never again ever touch or see my daughter on this earth.

The funeral was as beautiful as the visitation. All of Margo's young classmates were honorary pall bearers and lined the aisle as she was brought in. I didn't want the service to ever end. She was buried in a country cemetery. The small circle drive continued to fill with snow. One last time, I didn't want to let Margo go. I stood there looking over the field of white with snow falling and my daughter in a coffin. This was my new reality. I remember thinking, "Now what?"

I did continue, and do continue, to live my life, although it has changed because of my daughter's death. But I am forever better for having loved Margo. There is never a day that she isn't on my mind. The beauty is that now, rather than focusing on her death, I am able to focus on her life and her blessings that continue to unfold. I thank God for sharing Margo with me for twelve years of life and for eternity in my heart.

Meditation

Imagine that you are sitting by the side of a huge canyon. You look into the chasm before you. A river of tears far below flows through the canyon. You realize this canyon is the hollow place inside of you that cries out for your child.

As you sit there, an angel comes and places a soft, warm shawl around your shoulders and tells you that this is the mantle of divine compassion.

As you touch the soft shawl, the angel sits down beside you and holds your hand. You speak to the angel about your grief. As the two of you cry, your tears flow into the canyon's great river.

Now you look up and see a rainbow of hope beyond the canyon. With the angel's arm around your shoulder, the two of you gaze upon the rainbow.

Prayer

Divine Mother of those who grieve,
see here a broken-hearted one.
Relieve the ache of my anguished spirit.
Reach into the canyon of my weary soul
and lift my tears of sadness to your tender cheek.
Soothe my pain and comfort my sorrow.
Help me to accept the death of my child
and to have faith that _____ is at Home with you.
I turn to you in my time of great loss
and place my trust in your enduring love.

For Today

I will remember the gentle touch of divine
compassion.

CHAPTER THIRTEEN

We Had

Our Struggles

BY BARBARA H.

Gil and I were married for more than thirty years. It was a good match. We raised two children, Adam and Andrea. Both children live out of state. Andrea is married and has two children. We loved being grandparents and made several trips to California to play with those two boys.

Gil was a highly intelligent and very compassionate man. Part of what made us a good match was that we both loved to discuss social issues. The needs of others in our society were of great interest to both of us.

One of our tough challenges was Gil's addiction to alcohol. This disease caused considerable conflict in our marriage. After extensive professional help and Gil's inability to conquer this addiction on his own, he went to inpatient and then outpatient treatment. It's not surprising that his addiction and the ongoing process of his recovery greatly affected our marital relationship. During the time we struggled through his efforts at recovery, Gil and I never stopped working on bettering our relationship. The bond of love we shared was extremely important to both of us. We worked hard at deepening and strengthening this love.

One weekend I went to Centerville to take my eighty-five-year-old mother home. I stayed with her to get her settled. At that time, Gil and I decided to try living apart for a while in order to sort out some of the problems that caused tension for us. During the two days I was with my mother, I tried to call Gil several times but was unable to reach him. This didn't alarm me because it wasn't unusual for him to be away. Gil was a busy guy. He went often to visit the sick at a local care center and was involved in numerous other charitable activities.

When I returned home, I received a phone call telling me that Gil had been found dead of an apparent heart attack. This totally unexpected news completely stunned me. Although we were separated, I loved him very much.

It took a long time for Gil's death to become real to me because it happened so suddenly and without warning. I understood from this experience what others have said: "We can know something intellectually but still deny that it has happened, or fail to believe in our heart that it is true."

After Gil died, I thought about the difficulties we'd had when he was recovering from alcoholism and how we both made a great effort to not only save our marriage but to find new ways to care about one another. My good memories of Gil far outweigh the painful ones and I treasure each of the moments when we reached out to one another in an effort to grow closer.

My children provided a much-needed support to me after Gil died and were able to help me with lots of essential tasks, like sorting through his things. We were amazed at how many treasures we found; all the things he had written and saved that were meaningful to him. Gil was an avid reader and a deeply spiritual man. We found little sayings written on Post-it® notes that he had come across and that must have meant a lot to him.

Adam and Andrea went back to their homes a week or so after Gil died, and then I was left to face the loneliness and hollowness that comes after someone you love dies. I was lost. Initially I did as most do. I took care of the necessary business at hand and went through the motions of living. No matter what I was doing, I frequently expected Gil to come walking in the door during the day, or the phone would ring and my first thought was that it would be Gil calling.

There were countless ways in which I missed Gil. He died right after Christmas. When the winter snows came, he was not there to help me with things I had taken for granted, like cleaning the driveway. The evenings and weekends were especially lonely without him. I missed the long talks we often had about current issues and ideas. We were both active in peace and justice movements, and how I longed for him to be there to discuss these issues with me. We loved gardening together, and when it came time to work in the yard in the spring it just wasn't the same without Gil.

I made a great effort to adjust to my life without him, and worked hard at trying to be positive, but was amazed at how the tears would come when least expected. It would have been easy to just stay home, hide out, and let the world go by, but I knew it was important to carry on with the commitment that Gil and I had to the important concerns of society.

One of the enjoyable trips that Gil and I took every summer was to a cabin in the Colorado Rockies. The first summer after his death, I decided to make the trip without him, although I knew it would be a lonely time for me. It took a lot of courage to go there all by myself, but the grieving that I did while I was in the mountains was something that really helped me work through some of my pain and sadness. Making the effort to go there that first summer, facing the fact that I was alone and letting the tears come, enabled me to go again each summer with more peace and comfort.

I never dreamed that Gil would die quickly, with no warning, nor did I have an inkling of how extremely difficult life would be without my soul mate. Since his death, I have discovered more courage within me than I ever imagined possible. I try to be an active mother, grandmother, and master gardener, and to contribute as much as I can to my community. I continue to struggle with loneliness and with the reality that Gil is not coming back. I feel blessed to have had him for my husband. One of my greatest consolations is that, at the time of his death, he seemed to be closer to God and more at peace than he had been in years.

Meditation

Imagine that you and your loved one are standing in a beautiful place. God is standing there in the middle of the two of you and places an arm around each of your shoulders.

As the three of you stand quietly, you feel a tremendous love flowing between each of you. Whatever problems and struggles you may have had in the past no longer seem relevant.

You let yourself rest in the beauty of the love
between the three of you, knowing that all is
well.

Prayer

Dear God of unconditional love,
you know what lies within the human heart.
The life I once shared with _____
included some difficulties and challenges.
Now that he (she) is no longer with me,
I want to remember the positive things
and to let go of what caused us problems.
Soothe my sorrow and bring healing to my pain.
I will not let the memories of our struggles
keep me from remembering the goodness of our love.

For Today

I will carry a happy memory of my loved one
in my heart and find solace in this
remembrance.

CHAPTER FOURTEEN

I Feel Relief.

Is That Okay?

BY JUDY H.

I was forty-five years old when my mother developed cancer. Mom had continually complained of aches and pains and considered herself unwell for as long as I could remember. For most of her life, the relationship I had with her was less than I desired. My mother complained about everyone and everything, especially voicing her unhappiness about me, whom she constantly criticized.

During childhood, Mom often reprimanded me for being too loud when we had company, frequently reminding me how ashamed she was of me. No matter how hard I tried, I couldn't seem to be the daughter she wanted me to be. I never felt like I met her expectations. When I married, it was not surprising that Mom did not like the person I chose for a husband.

My mother suffered from depression and also tended toward self-absorption. This self-centeredness touched the lives of everyone in our extended family. She didn't enjoy being a grandmother, yet she grumbled that the grandchildren didn't stop by to visit her or give her enough attention. No matter how much people did for her, she was never satisfied.

We children felt sorry for our dad because our mother demanded a lot from him during their fifty-one years of marriage. In spite of the way she ordered him around, we never heard a complaint from him. In fact, from our perspective we thought he babied and pampered her, probably in order to keep peace in the family in whatever way he could. In the end, his attentiveness to Mom ended up being a much-needed gift when her cancer was discovered.

Medical tests revealed that extensive cancer in the colon had spread to her lungs. The doctors did not recommend chemotherapy or radiation because they felt it probably would not make a significant difference. As the cancer developed, my mother demanded that we children be with her constantly. We did what we could, trying to be caring and understanding of her impatient demands. We knew she was unaware of the time and energy that we also needed to give to our jobs and parenting. Fortunately, Dad was a good caregiver and Mom was able to be at home until the last six weeks before she died.

As Mom grew more ill, I tried to initiate conversations about our stormy relationship. I longed for both of us to find peace but my mother refused to talk to me about our differences, choosing instead to express her resentment about having cancer and about how hard life was for her. As the weeks went by, Mom was sedated with pain medication and conversation was no longer an option. I never had an opportunity again to talk about our relationship.

When Mom died, I felt a huge relief. This emotion was followed by guilt about feeling such relief. I questioned myself, "How can I feel this way when my mother has just died?" There was some sadness inside when I thought about not having a mother anymore and because I knew that my father was lonely. Mostly, though, I felt guilty because I experienced a great weight being lifted from me. This inner turmoil of relief and guilt kept me struggling to find peace.

With Mom's death, I recognized the finality and impossibility of ever bettering our relationship. Doubts arose as I questioned whether I had really tried my best to mend our differences. I had to admit that most of the time I had not liked my mother, although I did love her.

Eventually I found a grief support group, and this proved to be the gift I needed to sort through my emotional distress. I learned that I was not a bad person because of my feelings. My mother had been a difficult person and I had made every effort to be the best daughter I could be. After talking to a grief counselor, I realized that my mother responded to life the way she did because of how she felt about herself. This helped me to not only accept my mother, but to also feel a deep sorrow for Mom because she could not find happiness within herself.

I was finally able to feel more love for my mother than I ever had felt before. I knew that I tried to be as good to her as I could be. The best part was realizing that I really did love her. What brought me the most peace was believing that my mother was now the happiest she had ever been. Not only was she finally at peace, but so was I.

For those whose relationship with someone deceased has been a struggle and has not been resolved before death, I know how it can create a complicated grief process. When this happens, it's vital to get the help needed to resolve the inner conflict. Most of all, I've learned that it's okay to feel relief when someone close to us dies.

Meditation

Picture yourself at one of your favorite spots. You are there having a talk with God. Tell the Holy One about your feeling of relief, what it is like for you, and why you feel this way.

Recall and share the experiences you had with the person who died. Then, listen to what God speaks to you about your goodness and about your attempts to love this difficult person.

When your conversation is complete, accept the loving embrace of God and allow yourself to be at peace with your sense of relief.

Prayer

Heart of Abundant Love,
you know everything my heart contains.
Please take my questions and concerns
and wrap your merciful love around them.
Assure me of your understanding and care
as you help me sort out my mixed emotions.
I long to be at peace with my sense of relief
and the reprieve I feel regarding _____'s death.
Help me to let go of whatever causes me distress

and to look forward to the unfolding future.
Thank you for guiding me as I move on with my life.

For Today

I will allow myself to enjoy the relief I experience and be grateful that I can now let go of
what I could not repair.

CHAPTER FIFTEEN

No More Phone Calls

from Mom

BY JANET B.

My mom died when I was thirty-eight years old. We had an especially close relationship and her death was extremely difficult for me. Mom died on my birthday and that made it a bittersweet thing. In a way, it was an honor for someone I loved so much to die on my birthday, but in another way, my birthday will never be the same again. I can never celebrate another one without also remembering that I no longer have my mother with me.

I moved to California after I was out of high school two years and went to live with my sister who was four years older than I was. Mom really hated to see me move there and we used to talk on the phone almost daily. We both missed each other and found comfort in knowing we could be there for one another.

Sometimes we talked about something specific, but most of the time we just chatted. Five years after my sister and I moved away, Mom was still so lonesome for us that when my dad retired, the two of them moved to California so they could be with us. We all lived together happily and I would come home for lunch often so I could have extra time with them. Then, my sister married and moved to Iowa. When my parents discovered that my sister was pregnant and they were going to be grandparents, they felt the tug to return to Iowa in order to be near their new grandchild. Eventually, they moved back. When they did, it was really hard for me. I missed our times together. While I had friends, it seemed like no one understood me like my mom did. Fortunately, when she moved away, we picked up again on our regular phone conversations.

When my mother became seriously ill, those daily phone calls became increasingly important to me. I needed to hear her voice. After Mom passed away, I can't begin to describe how lost I felt. There were many times when I wanted Mom's advice. I ended up crying a lot because she wasn't there to listen and counsel me. I missed her a lot. When I needed to vent about tough stuff going on, I again cried with loneliness. When the kids did something funny, or got an award, I prayed that Mom was watching from above. She was a fabulous grandmother and absolutely loved to hear about the kids' accomplishments. I think this part is the hardest about not having my mother here. We shared everything.

I spent the last three weeks of Mom's life with her. I tried to remember to tell her everything I needed to say. Since her death, I still find myself going over and over those last three weeks in my head, and I'll often remember something I wish I had told her. I sometimes talk out loud to Mom. I hope she hears me.

One thing that comforts me is that I am sure she knows how much I loved her. I told her that every single time we talked. Once when she came to California to visit without my dad, I took her to the airport to go home. During the rush of getting her luggage out of the car and making sure she got to where she needed to be, I forgot to tell her that I loved her. Mom didn't have a cell phone and I panicked. I called the airport where she made her connection and had her paged. She didn't hear the page so I prayed that nothing would happen on her flight home. I never felt so unnerved in my life. Was I ever happy to hear her voice when she called to tell me that she got home safely! She just laughed at me and thought my concern was funny.

When I'm out shopping or at the grocery store, I'll see ladies who would have been my mom's age. Sometimes I strike up a conversation with them (they probably think I'm nuts) or I try to help them if they need assistance with something. Maybe I'll open the door for them, or let them go in front of me. Doing this somehow keeps me connected to my mother. I know she would have liked me doing that for someone and it feels good to help someone else's mother.

When I see women my age out with their moms shopping, or at lunch, or notice them in a car together, I look at them and wish I had mine with me. I pray they aren't taking advantage of their parents. I feel really sad when I see someone mistreating her mother in public. It takes every ounce of my being to not protect her mom, or to tell her to be respectful of her. I want to warn her that her mother won't be around forever.

I tried going to a grief counseling group. There were about fifteen women whose mothers had just died. The facilitator invited them to tell their stories and almost every single woman talked about how she wasn't very close to her mother, or that they had had a fight and her mother passed away before they could make amends. I couldn't believe my ears.

I felt sad for them, but I was also pleased to say that my mom was the greatest mother in the world and that I had the best relationship with her. She went from being my mom to being my best friend. After I left the group that time, I wondered if they resented me for saying what I did, but what I shared was the truth. I didn't go back to the grief support group again because it added to my sorrow for me to hear about those unloving relationships between the daughters and mothers.

Even though I was there during the last weeks to help my dad and sister as Mom prepared to go Home, I continue to struggle with not having my best friend to call when I just need to talk. I know it's going to take a long time before my loneliness leaves me. In the meantime, I'll continue to be grateful for the exceptional and beautiful relationship I had with my mother. I'll keep on talking to her in my heart because it makes me feel better.

Meditation

Choose a quiet place where you can sit and be with the memory of your mother. Think of some of your favorite remembrances of her.

Draw a heart on a piece of paper. Write on this heart the qualities of your mother that you most love and miss.

Hold this heart close to your own heart. As you feel your heart beat, let the qualities of your mother slip into your heart.

Renew your confidence that you carry a part of your mother with you each day.

Prayer

Mother of the Grieving,
rock me in the cradle of your care.
Soothe me in your arms of kindness.
Embrace me with nurturing love.
Hold me close to your divine heart
as I grieve the death of my dear mother.
When I am lonesome for her voice,
grant me a thought or word of comfort.
When I long for my mother's presence,
help me find serenity in my memories of her.

For Today

I will remember and live one of the qualities I admired in my mother.

CHAPTER SIXTEEN

Dad,

I Just Wanted Your Love

BY DIANE K.

My dad died ten months ago. The pain is still with me, but not as great. The tears still come, but not as often. It has been a tough year, but God has given me strength, peace, and a lot of things that cause me to give thanks.

My parents divorced when I was seventeen. It was a bitter divorce and the three of us kids were put in the middle. For the past twenty-five years my relationship with my dad was rocky. I'd compare it to being on a roller coaster.

He was remarried three times after he divorced my mom, so I have nine stepbrothers and -sisters. Through the changes of his wives and stepchildren I always felt like he put those nine stepchildren before his own children. This hurt me and I often felt sad, even angry. I felt I was being treated as an outsider. It was the worst feeling in the world. I so badly wanted Dad to love me and to be special to him. I longed for him to treat me like a daughter. It never happened that way. He was always busy trying to build relationships with his stepchildren and his different wives.

All three times that he remarried, the fathers of those children were either deceased or not involved. My dad did everything he could to be a father to them, even though most of them were grown up. It was more important to him to be a father figure to them than a father to us. I felt like we were "911" children; when one of his marriages would end, he'd call on us and we would be there to comfort him and help him pick up the pieces.

Then, one December he was diagnosed with cancer. I remember getting the call on December 24 telling us that Dad was being taken away in an ambulance. We met him at the hospital. He had many tests that week and on the twenty-ninth he learned that the tests all confirmed cancer in his liver and probably lungs. From that day on, our relationship changed. We went with Dad to the medical appointments, chemo treatments, and blood transfusions, and assisted him at home as much as his wife would allow. He even started making me feel special.

One day when my husband and I went to visit, Dad had me go alone out to the back patio with him while he smoked. I noticed his arm was swollen and mentioned it to him. He said, "It's been that way all day. I think you should call the hospice nurse." I asked, "Do you want me to call her right now on my cell phone?" He said, "Yes." Of course, I didn't hesitate a second. He seemed to want my husband and I to be the ones to do things for him.

Dad still used every bit of strength he had to be there for his stepchildren when they were around, but he would turn to his three children when he was in a crisis, afraid, or thinking about his life coming to an end. Another time when I called to see how he was doing, Charlotte (his then-wife) said he wasn't feeling well. When he got on the phone to talk to me, I said, "Dad, I hear you aren't doing so well." He explained, "No, I need to go to the hospital because I'm having pains around my heart." I urged him to go immediately: "Dad, I'll hang up and you have Charlotte take you right to the emergency room." I called my sister-in-law, left work, and drove to the hospital. Once again, I was there for him when he was most in need.

Dad requested one-on-one time with each of his three children. It seemed like he was acknowledging, for the first time in a long while, that we were important to him. His wanting to have private time with each of us meant so much to me, probably more than anything he could have done. During my visit, we sat out on the back patio watching the birds and talking. During our visit, I felt like I was the only one that mattered. As I drove home that evening, I cried all the way. The tears were sad and happy at the same time. I thought, "Why could we not have talked like this before now? Why did he have to be dying for me to get my dad back?" I was mad that I was finally getting a glimpse of having a father and knowing there was only going to be enough time for a glimpse of him.

At the same time, I was grateful that God had given the three of us the opportunity to draw closer to my dad and that we had accepted it. I was sad that his time on earth was just about over, and that it took his dying to have him be the dad that I had yearned for him to be for many years. I had longed for my children to have a close relationship with their grandpa. I wanted him to come and watch my son play football, to be proud of him and say, "That's my grandson." I wanted him to come and see my daughter show her sheep during the county fair and say, "That's my granddaughter." Even though I yearned for these things, I knew we were never going to do what I had dreamed of and there was nothing I could do to change that.

I have often envied the relationship that my husband and our daughter have. They are very close, and probably do not even realize how fortunate they are to have that relationship. Sometimes I wonder if it would have been easier if Dad had been dead, because to see your dad nearby and not have a relationship with him is terribly painful. I kept trying over the years to squeeze in between his stepchildren, hoping he would see me, but it never worked. Maybe he knew I loved him and felt he had to convince the others that he was worth loving.

However, with all of that said, God did allow us to be blessed with many beautiful memories to carry us through the sad, difficult times. Dad was able to retire and they had a nice retirement supper for him. His co-workers and supervisors said the most wonderful things about him. Dad truly loved working and made it a big part of his life. He was the kind of person who would give a complete stranger the shirt off his back, but would not have time for those who were his own children.

Dad stayed at his sister's house during radiation therapy treatments. We were able to spend lots of time with him while he was at my Aunt Joyce's house. He was in his own home the last weekend of his life. That Saturday night, my brother, sister, and I went with our families to help move him from the living room to the bedroom for the night. We all tucked him into bed. The love in the room that night was the most powerful love I have ever experienced in our family. It is difficult to describe.

We told stories, sang songs, laughed, and reminisced. Dad's youngest granddaughter and I sang "Rock-a-Bye Baby" to him just before we left. Without saying it, in the room that evening there was all the forgiveness that was needed and all of the love to make up for past years. God truly blessed us on Dad's next-to-last night of life, on his last time of being alert and aware of our presence. We truly knew how much he loved us and he knew how very much we loved him.

I learned through my journey with my dad that as we accompany those we love during their last steps on this earth, special memories and blessings come that can last us a lifetime. I now believe miracles do happen. Even on our deathbeds.

Meditation

Picture yourself as a small child in the arms of your trustworthy God.

Allow God to be the parent you missed in your own father or mother.

Let yourself be rocked tenderly in the soft cradle of the divine arms.

Hear God sing a little lullaby to you. Savor this experience.

Prayer

Sacred Kindness,
your heart is large enough to embrace each of us
who missed experiencing a father or a mother's love.
Today I forgive my father (mother) for his (her) failings,
for any way in which he (she) disappointed my expectations.
I open my heart to your all-embracing, plentiful kindness
and extend this unconditional love to my father (mother).
While I cannot undo the past or change what happened,
I can open my heart and offer pardon for his (her) weaknesses.
Thank you for the wideness of your mercy, gracious God.

For Today

The thought of God gently rocking me as a
child in need of comforting love will help to
soften any hardness in my heart.

CHAPTER SEVENTEEN

My Brother Died

a Violent Death

BY PATRICK J. M.

I'm a police and fire chaplain, so I routinely respond to violent crime calls, fire-related tragedies, and serious accidents. I'm also a licensed mental health practitioner. Dealing with complicated human problems is a day-to-day reality for me. I'm comfortable with problem-solving in an emotionally charged environment and people don't hesitate to call upon me for help when they need it.

Yet, when a phone call brought the news that my brother was killed in a violent crime at a shopping mall, all I could do was weep. As I learned more about the carnage of that day, my weeping became more volcanic, arising from an unexplored depth in my normally composed self and carrying me to the edge of insanity. My emotions didn't seem like me. Yet, it *was* me and it still is me—in the raw, unprotected by my usual coping mechanisms and my beliefs about the fairness of life. The event traumatized me. My deep well of resourcefulness ran dry.

The confirmed account of what happened is simple enough. An enraged nineteen-year-old man carried an AK-47 military assault rifle and two magazines of ammunition into a shopping mall. He entered a department store complex, took an elevator to the third floor, got out, and then opened fire on innocent Christmas shoppers. In his suicide note, he recorded that he wanted to be remembered as somebody *big*, since he had spent most of his life being victimized by others.

Eight innocent people died in less than six minutes. Many others were wounded and lay begging for help as the teenager fired away at the shoppers. My brother and his wife were at the courtesy counter waiting for Christmas gifts to be wrapped. My brother, John, age sixty-five, was killed near the counter while his wife, only several feet away, watched him die.

What do I see? What do I feel? What do I do to heal? It changes from day to day, even months after the traumatic event.

What do I know? It has taken time to put the pieces together, but the track of the killer now seems a little clearer. My brother died from one bullet in the leg and two bullets through his head. An AK-47 is designed for one purpose: to kill human beings. It shoots an unstable bullet, and as the bullet tumbles it shreds flesh and turns bones into powder. My brother lost his life as he tried to confront the killer in an effort to stop the shooting. The man must have panicked and killed himself after he murdered John. The police estimate that John's action saved the lives of fifteen to twenty others. Why did John try to intervene in the killing spree? I'll never know. Whatever his motivation, it cost him his life.

What do I feel? The nightmares still haunt me and some have become more haunting now, months after the event. In them, I see my brother's bright smile turn to bloody pulp as his head explodes from the AK-47 bullets. I wake up with a start, walk around for a while, try some water to quench my thirst, then sit still to calm myself with pleasant memories of John's work in peace and justice ministries.

I still weep at the images of a violent death for a person who abhorred violence and lived with gentleness. I'm afraid to go back to sleep because the nightmares refuse to stop working on me. My sense of loss is profound, but I know it is nothing like the feeling of loss his wife, children, and grandchildren feel. John was a unifying center of love for them.

What do I do? I still weep. Waves of sadness wash over me at times and I lose control. The waves often catch me by surprise. I warn people that I can't talk much about what happened. I've left dinner parties several times because the compassion of good friends stirs up too much emotion. I wonder if I'll ever recapture my old grounded presence, or if I'll ever find real rest.

I talk, at times, and that helps. I trust good friends with deep, honest sharing, but I still find it difficult to talk. I'm blessed with a good marriage and that's a safe place, but I sometimes relieve my wife of unnecessary burdens by asking her if it's okay to just be alone. Then I move into a welcome solitude and let the silence soothe my soul.

I pray, usually alone. I seek a now more hidden God, and I remain quiet in God's presence. I know that deep in this solitude, I'm in touch with John's spirit. My prayers are clearer, more focused, and inevitably turn to questions about *why* things happened the way they did. I have no answers, but I have learned to surrender to Divine mystery.

I study and reflect on deep truths, and these reflections give me access to a richer prayer life. I've been seriously studying what we Christians call "resurrection." I've read every sourcebook and commentary I can find. I arrive at a deeper understanding, small awareness by small awareness. I'm now clear that God will restore life in God's due time. That means John's flesh, my flesh; and we will be able to touch, embrace, and be brothers once more. I dream about going whitewater rafting with John again, or fishing, or just talking in an informed way. I find light and peace in these images.

When the peace fades and the darkness closes in again, I'm oppressed by images of what happened on the day my brother was killed and I don't know what to make of it. I'm not too sure what my reality is, except to be as compassionate as I can be for those who are victimized by violence.

Meditation

Sit in a place of comfort and assume a posture of ease.

Place your hand on your forehead. As you breathe in, visualize the painful images in your mind dissolving. As you breathe out, allow the dissolved images to evaporate. Repeat this for a while.

Place your hand on your heart. As you breathe in, visualize the sorrowful feelings in your heart dissolving. As you breathe out, allow the dissolved feelings to evaporate. Repeat this for a while.

Fold your hands on your lap and repeat the words "soothe me" on the in-breath and "heal me" on the out-breath.

Prayer

Divine Healer,
so much haunts my mind and floods my heart
as I think about the horrifying death of _____.
At times, grief threatens to consume me.
Calm my troubled thoughts and disturbed feelings.
Bring your peace to my wounded, hurting heart.
Help me to be gentle with the soreness of my spirit.
Remind me often that your compassionate love endures.
In the turmoil of the lingering images in my mind,
may your love steady me and guide me toward better days.

For Today

I will breathe out the oppressive thoughts
and feelings that flood my mind and heart.

CHAPTER EIGHTEEN

Being Single

Adds to My Grief

BY JANE M.

When I think about losing my mom four years ago, the grief is still almost suffocating.

Though our family was and is very close, my mom and I had a really special relationship. Losing her to cancer was just about the most devastating thing I could imagine.

My younger sister and I had both left home by the time Mom died and we were extremely worried about Dad, who was alone and without a job. As strange as it may sound, this was the closest I ever felt to my dad.

My sister had been dating her high school sweetheart for years and had someone there for her. So my dad and I relied on each other after Mom's death. He was the only one who could empathize with my grieving alone in an empty house. It was comforting to know I wasn't the only one doing this by myself.

Six months later, my dad starting dating Anne after meeting her through a grief support group. Two years later they were married. Not only did I lose my mom, but I felt like I lost the special relationship that I was building with my dad before he remarried. Once he started dating Anne, she took over all the duties of caring for him and making sure he was okay.

This was a difficult period when I fought with my dad and said things I never thought I'd say. I don't regret them, but they were harsh and extremely hurtful. I was worried that he was dating too soon and furious that I would have to share family time with a stranger, especially in such early stages of grief. Anne is a great woman, but her presence challenged the new dynamic of our family. It complicated the situation since she was still grieving her first husband who died a year to the day before my mom died.

Anne and her husband couldn't have children—which was both a blessing and a curse for my family. On the positive side, no kids meant there were fewer people to blend together. The difficult part was that it caused miscommunication and frustration many times as Anne learned to share her husband with his two daughters, whom Dad declared would always be more important than she would be to him.

As much as we believed Dad, we also knew we had to share our time with Anne. We couldn't begrudge his need to have a partner. After having an exceptionally functional, healthy, loving family for twenty-four years, I had no idea how to deal with the new circumstances that I resented so deeply. Time has helped to ease my resentment and my relationship with Anne has slowly improved, but it is still difficult to know exactly what role she plays in our family life.

As a side note, I hate the word "stepmom" because it implies my parents were divorced when really they had a strong and happy marriage. There should be another word to mean "my-dad's-wife-who-is-here-only-because-my-mom-is-dead" but, for now, stepmom will have to do.

My dad and Anne's wedding, as well as my sister's a month earlier, were joyous occasions, but they left me feeling even more alone, and angry that I was having to deal with the evolving stages of grief (not to mention everyday stresses) by myself. Questions plagued me that I tried not to acknowledge, given how selfish and irrational they seemed: "When will I have someone to help me get up when I feel like I can't do it anymore? Who will support me through the waves of grief that come without warning? Who will love me when I am sick with the ovarian cancer I am superstitiously sure I will inherit from my mother?"

Of course, I have wonderful relatives and friends who love and care for me, but it does not seem the same as having a husband or boyfriend. The question I still ask is why God hasn't brought someone into my life to be my partner and companion. Some suggest that I must still have lessons to learn, but I look at my dad and sister who have wonderful spouses *and* lots of issues to still work through and lessons to learn, so that answer seems trite at best. It's hard not to get discouraged and overwhelmed. I recently experienced anxiety attacks after going back to my home of origin and having my time there feel completely normal without my mom. That normalcy momentarily crippled me and made the regular stress of my life unbearable. I wonder if I would have broken down like I did if I had a partner to talk to and to comfort me.

I know that a husband won't make my grief disappear. I even worry that I won't be able to open up to a partner who didn't know my mom and who might die young, too. Grief is so difficult and I would never claim that mine is worse than someone else's, but it is a unique experience to lose a parent without having a family of your own.

Meditation

Find a comfortable chair to sit in. If possible, put your feet up. Open your heart to an awareness of God's love being with you at this very moment.

As you sit quietly, allow this love to touch the places of your inner self that are hurting and lonely.

Close your eyes, breathe slowly and deeply. Continue to absorb God's love. Be at peace.

Prayer

God of Consolation,
at times life feels terribly unfair to me.
I shouldn't have to bear my grief alone
but right now that is how it is with me.
Please help me find a way to tend my pain
without someone close by to ease my sorrow.
May your abiding, loving presence
reassure me that I am never totally alone.
Bring comfort and solace to my heartache.
Soften the harsh reality of my aloneness.

For Today

I will visualize God as the companion who understands my sorrow and stands by me in this difficult period of my life.

CHAPTER NINETEEN

Seven Children,

No Time to Grieve

BY NAN G.

My husband Greg was an amazing man. You may think I'm biased, but ask anyone who knew him. Greg was an upbeat, optimistic person who loved life. As a social worker, he cared a lot about anyone who needed help. His job gave him the opportunity to work with troubled young people and he really liked being able to do this. Greg gained tremendous satisfaction from knowing he could make a difference in the lives of these young people. He was overjoyed whenever he saw their attitudes improve after he had worked with them.

Greg also loved being a dad. No amount of commotion bothered him, and he could make fun out of almost anything. When he came home from work at night, he'd start honking his car horn about the time he turned the corner by our street, to let our children know that he was coming. The kids would meet him at the driveway, and by the time they all came into the house they would be dancing, singing, and giggling.

We had just found out that we were expecting our seventh child. That day Greg called to tell me that he was going out to check on a young person and the house-sitter after receiving a phone call about the situation. I didn't hear from Greg again for several hours. I tried to call his cell phone with no luck. My office called to say that DCI (Iowa's Division of Criminal Investigation) had stopped by our office looking for me. As soon as I picked up the kids from day care I went straight home. As I pulled into my driveway I saw a truck pulling in behind me. The driver told me not to go into the house. I was asked to follow them to the police station.

The next thing I knew I was being told that Greg had been killed by his client when he entered the house. The shock that I felt is beyond description. The whole thing was a nightmare, something that no one ever thinks they will really have to live.

How do you tell your children that their dad, whose liveliness and fun-loving spirit brought them daily joy, has just been killed? I explained to the children the best I could that someone had shot Daddy and that he would not be coming home again. The oldest child was nine-and-a-half and the youngest only one year.

We got through the funeral with the help of relatives and close friends, but all that is just a big blur in my mind. There were many, many people at Greg's funeral. Some of the young people with whom he had worked witnessed as to how he had changed their lives. One boy spoke about not having any hope until he started seeing Greg and how his life changed forever because of Greg's help.

With six young children and the seventh on the way, my life seemed pretty overwhelming without my partner and best friend to be there with me. I remember not wanting to think at all. I felt like "just tell me where to go and what to do." Fortunately, Greg's brother very quickly started coming at least two evenings a week to help with the children. My sister was also a great help.

We have a group of friends and they did whatever they could. Our church friends also offered support. They brought meals, and just did things that they saw needed doing. When people asked me how they could help, it was difficult for me to identify what needed to be done. My brain was lost in a fog. It took all my effort to force it to work, to keep myself together for the children. I knew it was important that they have the security of the strong family unit they were used to. It was all I could do to be there for them in as calm and reassuring a manner as I could manage.

As I anticipated having the child I was expecting without Greg, my heart felt like it would break. My sister wanted to go with me when I went into labor and a very good, longtime friend, Jeannie, also accompanied me to the hospital. The three of us got through it, but the void I felt without Greg's presence was excruciating. I gave birth to a beautiful baby girl and then home I went to again face family life without my husband.

People often ask me how I keep going with the huge responsibility of being an only parent and all that goes with it, while also dealing with the pain of grief. I tell them that I can't let myself think about the loss very much. You might say that I'm living in denial. Maybe that's true but it's all I can do, and it's what works for me. I don't have time to grieve and cry a lot because my children need me. So I pretend Greg is just gone for now and that it is temporary. This gets me through each day.

It's been said that we have to grieve our loss, but my grieving has to wait for me to raise my children. We mention Daddy a lot and they share their sadness whenever they want to. We talk about what Dad would do if he were here and they certainly bring him into much of our daily life with their conversations about him. Several years after Greg was killed, the governor of our state declared March 11 as "Greg Gaul Day" in Iowa because Greg had supported so many families and was "a respected member of the social work community who gave his life serving his client." My children and I have wonderful memories of their father and this tribute assures us each year just how special he was.

I am definitely aware that it's a couples' world, but that's okay with me, as I have my work cut out for me. I'm not a bit interested in a relationship at this time. Being a full-time mom leaves no thought or time for anything else. My women friends are understanding and sensitive to this aspect of my life. They have a night out with me every once in a while to make sure I have something of a social life.

Probably the most difficult part is watching the children grow up and not being able to see Greg enjoy their talents. I believe Greg is here and that he is not missing anything. We are the ones who don't get to see how he cherishes all of us. That was the best part about knowing Greg: it wasn't just living with him; it was seeing the world through his eyes that made it so great!

Meditation

Close your eyes and picture yourself with Jesus.
He looks upon you with great love and senses

how tired you are. Listen to him speak these words to you: "Come to me, you who are weary and carrying heavy burdens, and I will give you rest" (Mt 1:28). Now picture yourself leaning on Jesus, resting your head on his shoulder. Allow yourself to be comforted and renewed in strength.

Prayer

O Divine Comforter,
I come to you with an over-full life,
one that leaves me little time to grieve.
Please help me to bear my heavy burdens
and do what I can to tend my sorrow.
I will rest my weariness upon your heart
and trust that my grief will wait for me
until I am able to be attentive to it.
All I can do right now is lean on your love.
May your strength sustain me in my loss.

For Today

I will take little pauses during the day and draw strength from the Holy One's love.

CHAPTER TWENTY

I Miss My Grandma

BY MIKAYLA B.

My grandma was unable to move around very much without help for about four years. This was especially difficult for her because she really enjoyed her independence. Grandma didn't like having to rely on her family to get up and down or walk, but we loved assisting her. After those four years of being unable to do much to help herself physically, she developed cancer in her pancreas and liver. Once this happened, the cancer spread quickly. Grandma only lived a few months after being diagnosed.

When Grandma passed away, it was sort of a relief for those of us who loved her. She was never a burden for us; rather, our relief came from knowing that she no longer had to experience being uncomfortable with her dependency upon us. We knew that she did not like needing to have help all the time and that she often felt she was imposing on us. Her death meant she was now free from pain and discomfort. She didn't have to rely on my grandpa and the rest of us to assist her in getting around anymore.

I reminded myself that Grandma was now with her parents and other family and friends. I kept telling myself, "She is in a better place," but no matter how much I tried to convince myself of how much better off Grandma was since her death, it didn't seem to soften my grief one single bit. I still felt like someone had ripped a part of my heart away. Even though I was surrounded by people who cared about me, there was no one who could ease my sorrow. I felt even more alone in my sadness because when people tried to comfort me with their words, it was like none of them said the right things. My friends didn't know what might be helpful to console me because they still had their grandmas and grandpas. They didn't understand what it was like to no longer have a dear grandmother.

Everything reminded me of Grandma. I'd see something that was a part of her life or something she had given to me and I'd miss her again. When my neighbors had their grandmas visiting them, this increased my sadness. Seeing them together reminded me that Grandma would never visit me again. What caused the greatest sorrow was seeing how sorrowful my mom was about her mother's death. I would watch Mom cry and wonder what it was like to have your mom die. When I thought about that, I really felt bad because I didn't want my mom to die and leave me like Grandma did.

Eventually, I was able to talk about my grandma without crying hysterically, but I knew there would be times in my life when I would still be overcome with tears. On the anniversary of her death, I was once again reminded of the extreme heartache and sorrow I felt on the day of her death. Then I realized that I had made it through one year without her. Sure it was a rough year, and at one point I thought the sad feeling would never end, but it did lessen. That thought helped me and after that anniversary I began thinking that my grief would get easier. And it did, little by little.

Then my grandpa came to visit. As everyone else steadily got through their grief, he seemed to become worse with every day and began to get sick whenever he came to our home. He had never been sick when he and Grandma visited. After her death, he never seemed happy. There was a quiet loneliness about him. Seeing Grandpa like that made me feel my own pain all over again. In time, I began talking to my mom about everything that troubled me about my grandma's death. She listened to me and this helped, so I talked to Mom more and more. It also seemed to help Mom when we spoke about Grandma and when we both shared how much we missed her.

Every time I saw a picture of Grandma, heard something about her, or saw my grandpa so depressed, I was reminded of how sad I felt, too. I knew that I needed someone or something other than my mom to help me. Mom did help, but she was so close to the sorrow and I didn't always feel better after talking with her because of the sadness she carried in her heart. I didn't want to meet with a therapist or a counselor, even though people assured me this would help. I was hesitant to express something so personal to someone I didn't know. I kept trying to talk to my friends, but they didn't really understand why I felt so sad. I guess they thought I should have gotten over the death of my grandma right away.

Then, as if on cue, an absolute angel came into our lives. She knew what to say to us when we felt angry or sad. Sometimes she didn't say anything. She just listened as we talked about how much we missed Grandma. She encouraged us to tell stories about Grandma and to remember everything we could about her. This wonderful woman helped us all in ways I don't even understand to this day. She was so wise and was able to bring back the happiness in my grandpa that I had not seen in a long, long time. With her help, I was able to see that it was time for my grandma to leave us and that death is not a bad thing. Our angel helped us understand that we will all die someday and that Grandma went to a good place where she is happy and at peace.

I finally realized that I wasn't being a bad person because I continued to miss my grandma. I learned that it was natural for me to long for her because I loved her so much. I would always miss her because I was human. I also learned that, even though being sad is a natural part of grief, being sad all of the time is not helpful. What really helps is to look for the positive parts in life. It is even possible to look for the positive in the death of a loved one. Finding something positive when someone dear leaves us is one of the hardest things to do, but looking for it helps us to let go of our sorrow. At first, it seems impossible to think of anything favorable about the loss, but eventually we can find something positive there.

The positive that I discovered in Grandma's dying is that now she can walk and run again. She doesn't have to depend on someone else to help her do it. She can do whatever she wants to do. I'm so happy for Grandma and the freedom she now has in her new life.

My grandma had a special love for cardinals, so every time I see one of those red birds I feel like I am with her. She will be in my heart always. I will forever be proud to be her granddaughter.

Meditation

Sit next to a lamp that will allow you to feel the warmth from its light. If it is a sunny day, sit outdoors in the sun instead of by the lamp, or sit by a window with rays of sunshine streaming in.

The warmth extending from the light is like the rays of love streaming from your grandmother's love. Close your eyes and turn your face up toward the light. Imagine the light and warmth in your grandmother's heart shining on you.

As you experience this warmth, recall some aspects of your grandmother that you especially miss. Let her love shine into your heart. Feel her presence dwelling there with you.

Prayer

Divine Light,
thank you for my wonderful grandmother.
Even though it was time for her to die
I can't help wishing she was still here with me.
Help me find the positive even when I'm sad
and to recall the many things she taught me.
When I am tearful, bring her cheer into my heart.
Lead me to those who will listen to my grief
and who can comfort me when I am in need.
Thank you for giving me my grandmother.

For Today

I will take the warmth of my grandmother's
love with me into each part of my day.

CHAPTER TWENTY-ONE

My Husband

Took His Life

BY KATIE M.

As a young child, I visited the cemetery where my grandparents were buried and spied a grave set apart from the rest of the gravesites. When I asked why that person was way out there, my aunt explained that it was probably someone who died and could not be buried in holy ground. Of course that elicited more questions. She said, "We'll talk about it when you're older."

Several years later, my parents told me about a man from the parish who had died by suicide. The

Church considered it an unforgivable sin and there was a question as to whether he could be buried from the Church. I thought of that lonely grave up at the cemetery and wondered if that was where he would be buried. As I grew older, I was uncomfortable with the scripture reading of Judas's betrayal of Jesus and the words, "It would have been better if he had never been born (Mk 14:21)." These incidents were imprinted on my soul and reinforced by my church and society.

After graduating from college, I taught school and met the love of my life, Matthew, who was beginning his new job after graduating from law school. After a two-year courtship we married. Later we were blessed with five children.

When the first stages of Matt's depression appeared, he felt ashamed and worried for feeling that way. He knew the ravages of depression because his mother and sister suffered from it. He didn't want anyone to know he was having similar symptoms. I finally convinced him to see a doctor, who prescribed antidepressants, which helped Matt immensely.

Our lives were filled with family, friends, growing children, and renewal activities in our church. Matt was appointed a judge and I returned to my teaching profession. He was seeing a doctor and taking antidepressants, and we were in counseling. Although Matt had no major incidents, his depression sapped a lot of joy from his spirit and our lives.

In 1987 Matt suffered a major clinical depression requiring hospitalization and a six-month medical leave from his job, but he recovered so completely that we thought the depression was behind us. Those were good years for our marriage and family. Our children graduated from college, got married, and gave us our first grandchildren, who brought us much joy. Life seemed almost perfect.

During late fall and winter of 2000, Matt's depression returned with a vengeance. He visited his doctor regularly, took his medicine, and took a medical leave from his job. He shared his feelings of hopelessness with me, his fears that this time he could not shake the depression, that something terrible would happen. He would say things that broke my heart: "It doesn't matter who I am with, what I am doing, where I am, nothing helps, I'd just like to jump out of my skin and I can't. Every day is dark and black even when the sun is shining."

On May 8, 2001, I left the house to be with my sister, who was having medical tests. I knew Matt was not feeling well; he told me was going to lie down since he hadn't slept well that night. I suggested he take a walk, assuring him I would call later and see how he was doing. He told me he would probably take the phone off the hook (which he often did if he took a nap). I tried to call Matt several times while I was out but the line was always busy. I began feeling uneasy. I tried to dismiss it, thinking he was either still sleeping or had already gone for his walk.

When I arrived home the front door was locked. This raised a red flag for me. My heart beat quickly as I opened the door and called, "Matt." The smoke alarms and carbon monoxide monitor were all going off loudly. The house was filled with fumes. I raced down the steps to the attached garage. Matt was sitting on the front seat of the passenger side of the running car with his hands in his lap. He looked peacefully asleep, still in his pajamas. I grabbed hold of him, screaming his name, but he did not answer me. I knew he was dead.

The rest of the day was a blur. Many people came, bringing their love, support, sympathy, and offers of help and food. All I wanted was to feel Matt's arms around me, offering his assurance that everything would be all right, and for him to convince me that this was not really happening. How could this be? We didn't even have a chance to say good-bye; now he was gone forever. My mind and heart were filled with so many memories of our forty-two years together. I would never see him or hear his voice again. It was too much to comprehend or imagine. An overwhelming sense of loneliness swept over me.

Suicide carries a stigma and has a curiosity attached to it. People drove slowly by our house, pointing and looking. Many people don't understand depression. This can lead to ill-timed remarks and questions. Some people avoided me. To this day some have never even mentioned Matt to me. It is almost like he never existed.

Another byproduct of suicide is guilt. All kinds of thoughts ran through my mind: "If only I had stayed home with him that morning. If only I had loved him more, he would never have wanted to leave me." I worried about where he was now. Was he safe, at peace? I wanted to know he was not still in torment. Those old images from my childhood and youth kept recurring, even though I thought my image of God had evolved over the years. I had believed in a God of love, but now I was beginning to doubt God. Those words in scripture about Judas hung over me: "It would have been better if he had never been born." At times they would haunt me, but then I would remember our five wonderful children and eleven grandchildren and know that this was not my God.

Another aspect of suicide grief is seeing your children suffer profoundly because of the way their father died. We were all devastated. Matt would never consciously do anything to hurt us, yet, through his actions, he did. He thought he was sparing us from the suffering his depression was bringing upon his family.

I never felt anger toward Matt. I knew the deep darkness and suffering that was a part of his life for many years. I did feel a great sadness that he felt suicide was his only way to escape, and I was angry that he had to suffer from depression.

Today I feel, in the depth of my being, that Matt's death was, for him, the final healing after years of struggle. My healing is ongoing. It is a process of growth, knowing myself, accepting others' broken-ness—my own included—and understanding the depth and pervasive darkness of depression. Healing for me is also a process of surrender to and acceptance of Matt's death, with all the implications that the absence of his presence means for me and our family for the rest of my life. I miss Matt profoundly; I pray for him daily; and I know that he is at peace and all is well.

Meditation

Find a window where you can stand alone and not be interrupted. Notice how you can see through the window to what is beyond. Now close the curtain or pull the blinds. Observe how the view is completely blocked. Imagine how your loved one could not see a way out of his (her) situation.

Bring your loved one to mind. With loving compassion, draw him (her) close to your mind and heart. Have him (her) speak to you about the pain that led to suicide.

Open the curtain or pull the blinds. Gaze out the window. Visualize your loved one free and joyful, completely at peace. Allow your mind and heart to also be at peace and free from pain.

Prayer

God of the Desolate,
as your Son hung on his cross of excruciating pain,
he questioned whether you had abandoned him.
My loved one also grew desperate and felt defeated
as he (she) hung on the dark cross of hopelessness.
Now _____ is at Home in your heart of love.
Do not allow me to be overcome with guilt.
Free me from the grasp of aching remorse.
Grant me strength to remain firm in your love.
Heal me from the grief of my loved one's death.

For Today

Each clear window will remind me of the peace my loved one has found. Each clear window will also remind me that my peace can be restored as I heal from my grief.

CHAPTER TWENTY-TWO

She Was

My Best Friend

BY KAREN T.

Death is no stranger to me. I've lost my grandparents, parents, aunts and uncles, my husband, a baby at birth, a sister-in-law, and many friends. I miss them all greatly, but I'm going to tell you about losing my best friend, Caryl. When we have family members die, people offer a lot of sympathy. They can relate to our loss because of their own deceased relatives. I don't think most people understand how significant it is to have a best friend die. Sometimes his or her death hurts almost as much as that of someone in your own family.

Caryl was in a terrible auto accident the day before Thanksgiving. Her death was overwhelming and such a shock to me. I am having a hard time writing about this even now. I was out of town when it happened and my son called to tell me. When he said "Mom, Caryl died," I could not believe what I was hearing. At first, I hardly comprehended his words. Then I went down to the floor. My mind and heart couldn't handle what I was being told. I just kept saying "NO! NO!" It was so difficult to believe—to think that she was gone out of my life that fast. No time to prepare. No time to say goodbye. No "I love you." (Although I know that she knew I loved her.) I still find it hard to believe that she is gone. It's a terrible shock to have someone die in such a tragic way.

The last time I was with Caryl was over a month before she died because I was out of the country on a four-week vacation. I can't remember where the two of us were when I last saw her, but I know we laughed and had a good time. We always did. At the news of her death, I felt like I had wasted that whole month away and lost time with her that I could never get back. There are things you cannot do over and wish you'd done differently when someone dies so suddenly.

Caryl was a gentle person and had so much life to live, so much to give. She was the sister I never had. She lived two blocks away from me. We were walking partners, in a weekly prayer group, and vacationed together with friends, but the central core of our friendship was our deep connection whether we were together or apart.

I feel that Caryl and I were soul mates destined to meet. We laughed and cried together, and knew we had that deep soul-bonding. We were first introduced to each other at a "Monday Prayer Group" of women. I liked her right away. Her smile, her giggle, and her kindness were easy to love. When you see someone every week, you can get really close.

When Caryl's husband developed cancer a few years later, we especially connected because my husband died of cancer, too. We talked so much about Caryl's husband and their life together, and of what would eventually happen. Talking came so easy for us. She knew I understood what she felt and how hard it was. When he died, we grew even closer. Caryl knew that I had walked in her shoes.

Friendship is such a gift to give each other. Our walks gave us much pleasure. We talked all the time and both felt better for the time we had together. We could tell each other anything and had that unconditional love that is sometimes experienced with maybe one best friend, if we're lucky. I miss her great laugh, her smile, and her spirit. But I believe that her spirit is with me always.

When I got home after the news of Caryl's death, her family asked me to be one of the pallbearers for her funeral. Their request took my breath away. So much pain in my heart, but it was such a blessing to be able to do one final thing for her. I was honored, and yet, it was so hard to carry my best friend to her final resting place. I had never been a pallbearer before and didn't realize how heavy a casket is or how emotional carrying it would be. I'm proud that I was able to offer one last gift to my friend, but it was really a gift to me.

After Caryl died, a group of her friends and I got together to talk about our relationship with Caryl. We remembered all the good times we'd had. We laughed and cried as we shared our stories, but in the end we decided that it is very difficult to express what is deepest in our hearts.

Last Christmas some of her friends and I helped Caryl's daughter put up the tree and hang her mom's traditional decorations because her three siblings were coming to Caryl's home for one last Christmas. We went all through the house remembering Caryl. It was at that time that her daughter found a bag with a Christmas gift in it for me. The tag read: "To Karen, Love Caryl." It was a book: *Angels Everywhere*, by Lynn Valentine.

This is a quotation by an unknown author in the book that Caryl meant to give me:

"Whisper of Angel Wings"

Today I stumbled and once again was lifted up
by an unseen hand.

What comfort and joy that knowledge brings
for I hear the whisper of angel wings.

The guardian angels God sends to all to bear us
up when we stumble and fall.

Trust him, my friend, and often you'll hear the
whisper of angel wings hovering near.

I am comforted to know that Caryl is my personal
guardian angel and that she is always there by me. I
can see her smile and hear her giggle now. In all my
sadness, I know how lucky I am to have known someone who makes it hard for me to say goodbye.

As I write this, a year has passed since Caryl's
death. It's still tough not to be able to see and visit
with her, but having one of her daughters living close
by to spend time with and to talk to about Caryl has
helped me with my grief.

Caryl, I will keep you in my heart always. Thanks
for being my best friend. You enriched my life.

Meditation

Make a list of the qualities you valued in your
good friend. Make another list of the experiences
of your friendship that are especially memorable
for you.

Place both in a small box and gift-wrap it.

Set the box in a place where you will be reminded of the gift you had in this dear friend. Take a
moment from time to time to hold the gift box
with a spirit of gratitude.

Prayer

Bestower of Friendship,
I want to deny the death of my good friend.
I'd like to turn my back on this harsh reality.
Yet, death has truly claimed _____.
It's going to take time before I can fully grasp my loss.
Hold me close to your caring, compassionate heart
until my whisper of acceptance becomes stronger.
Encircle me with strength when I miss her (his) presence.
Remind me that my friend lives on in my heart.
Help me to take one day at a time. That is enough for now.

For Today

I will honor and live one of the special
qualities that I valued in my friend.

CHAPTER TWENTY-THREE

How Can There Be

Someone Else with Dad?

BY JANET B.

I was concerned about my dad. How was he going to cope with my mom's death? Alone in the house all the time. Winter was coming. I could picture him in the basement, getting depressed.

He golfed almost daily the first two years after Mom died but then didn't seem to find satisfaction in it anymore. Dad also did some remodeling around the house but now he seemed unable to fill his days with activity. I called nearly every day, more for me than for him. I wanted to make sure he was all right. I couldn't fully grasp the pain he was in.

Thankfully, I knew longtime friends Don and Maryanne were there for him. I knew they would help him function, but I also knew he would not want to be the third wheel in their marriage. But, as good friends do, they forced him to go out and be with them socially.

One Memorial Day weekend, he planned to attend his high school reunion as he and Mom had done every year. He called when he got home, told me he had had a fun time, and that he had asked a very nice lady named MJ to have dinner with him. He sounded like a school boy as he explained how he had just blurted out the invitation to her. He was embarrassed at the way he did it, but I was glad Dad was going to have a companion to be with when he went out. I didn't think anything of it.

In July, we had a family reunion. I was looking forward to seeing all my aunts, uncles, and cousins that I had not seen in a long, long time. Those family reunions were always a blast. What a great family! Dad let me know that he had invited MJ to our family reunion. "Hmmm," I thought. "Why?" But I ignored my emotional response. When she arrived, I noticed that Dad was quite affectionate toward her. I went over and greeted her and went on my way. After the reunion we all went to Dad's home. When it was time for MJ to leave, my sister commented, "I wonder if he's going to kiss her?" I blurted out "No! Why would he kiss her?" We all watched from the window . . . no kiss. So I knew I was right. Although he continued to ask MJ out on dates, I felt fine about that.

September rolled around and Dad came to California for my birthday and the anniversary of my mom's death. I picked Dad up from the airport and we had a great drive to my house, chatting all the way. As we came into the house, he blurted out, "I asked MJ to marry me." My heart started to pound and tears rolled down my face. We talked and talked but I couldn't hear a word he was saying. All I could think about was how Mom would feel. I couldn't possibly like MJ anymore because she would take the place of my mother.

My dad was moving on. He was happy. He and I didn't share "that pain" in common anymore. I was being left behind in my misery. I was two thousand miles away from my hometown and alone. None of my friends had lost their parents. Nobody knew what I was feeling.

Each time we talked on the phone, Dad sounded happier. He continually tried to help me realize and appreciate what it was like for him. But all I could think of was that we were cheating on Mom.

That period of my life was a difficult time for me. I tried so hard to "understand." I'm a grown adult but I couldn't "just feel happy" for my dad. Trust me, I wanted to. I told him that I had a mature side and a not-so-mature side of my brain. The mature side wanted to see him happy again, but the not-so-mature side wanted him to emotionally stay with me, to be sad with me. Each time we had a conversation, he would talk about his new life, how happy he was, how excited he was to get married and start a new life. That was like sticking a knife right through my heart. I wasn't happy. I wasn't starting a new life. I hated those three months of my life. Everyone was happy for Dad and MJ except me. I kept asking myself, "Why can't I get on board?" Again, there was no one to talk to as none of my friends had gone through that sort of experience. I just wanted to curl up in bed and sleep, to forget about what was going on around me.

Then the wedding came. I knew I had to be happy for Dad, but I'm not the best at keeping my feelings inside. As the wedding day drew near, I had an abundance of tears. The night before the wedding, our families got together for the first time. We had dinner at my new stepbrother and sister-in-law's home. We blended like we'd been together forever. That was amazing and I thought, "Okay, this is not going to be so bad."

Then, the morning of the wedding came. It seemed like I could feel every nerve ending in my body. How was I going to hold it together? Boy, did I talk with Mom a lot that day! There were many family members around but I couldn't hear anything anyone was saying. I was too focused on "keeping it together" for Dad. I think I did pretty well. I knew Dad was happy again.

The next event was their first trip to California as a married couple. This was in September, again at the time of my birthday and the anniversary of Mom's death. Wow, was I nervous. We were going to be in my house together for eight days. I would have nowhere to run and hide.

I didn't have anywhere for them to stay, so my husband and I remodeled the house and gave them their own bedroom. I decorated and tried to make it comfortable. I even put their wedding picture on the side table. I knew I had to put forth some effort. That is what my mom would have wanted me to do. By the time I picked Dad and MJ up from the airport, my stomach was horribly upset. I would have to actually see them "together," kissing and holding hands. They would go to the same bedroom. Their closeness was going to be in my face twenty-four-hours-a-day, for eight days. How was I going to handle it? I kept telling myself, "Be a big girl. You're a grown adult. Get over this. Dad is happy and that is all that matters." But none of that worked. I was just a mess.

Now that I look back on that time, it was rather funny. I think MJ was just as nervous as I was. A side of me came out that I was proud of, if I do say so myself. I tried very hard to make her feel comfortable. She tried her best to help me be at ease. I watched her interact with my kids. She was wonderful. I watched her relate with my dad. She was equally wonderful. I could tell she was concerned for my feelings. As the days went on, the tensions eased. I actually started to enjoy their visit. It was a pleasant surprise.

My dad and I always went to the beach and then to lunch to celebrate my birthday. MJ didn't want to go because she thought it was "our day." Dad and I finally got her to go and we had a great time. We talked about Mom and about MJ's late husband the whole time. It was a weird but very nice day.

After their visit, I turned a corner on my feelings about Dad's marriage and knew that all would be well. I'm glad I gave MJ a chance. I don't think my dad could have found a better person to live with for the rest of his life. She's the most caring and understanding person I have ever met. And I know that as a result of this relationship, my daddy is going to live a long, long time.

Thank you MJ, for coming into our lives.

Meditation

Find a knife and two forks. Set the knife and one fork in front of you. These two items represent your father and mother. Pause to remember them as a couple and as your parents.

Now remove the fork and put it on the floor as a sign of the death of your mother (father). How is it for you to be without this part of your life?

Next to the knife, add the second fork as a sign of
the new person who is now in your parent's life.
How is it for you to have this individual enter into
a relationship with your father (mother)?

Close your eyes. Picture this new couple and
yourself joining hands while you are being surrounded by God's love.

Prayer

Patient and Caring God,
how do I cope with this situation I do not want?
Help me be attentive to my emotional responses
and to be tolerant with the part of me that resists.
Keep my mind and heart open and ready to grow.
With your love I can extend a genuine welcome,
even though a big part of me wants to turn away.
Assure me that the love I have for my deceased parent
will not lessen or be dishonored by a new relationship.
May I help contribute to the well-being of our family.

For Today

I will not give in to the part of me that resists
accepting my father's (mother's) newly found love.

CHAPTER TWENTY-FOUR

I Feel

So Guilty

BY MARIE R.

I'll never forget the day the phone call came telling me that my twenty-three-year-old brother had drowned in a fishing accident. I remember exactly what I was doing—standing in the kitchen putting the dough for chocolate chip cookies on the baking trays—and I can still recall each word that announced his death. I was twenty-five at the time and stunned by the horrible reality that someone in my family had died. Soon after my shock, an intense sadness followed. With it came a crushing sense of guilt as my mind overflowed with memories of my brother and myself in high school.

The more those memories played in my mind, the greater the remorse I felt over how I had treated him during the time we were together. Along with the guilt came a ton of regrets, especially that I had never asked his forgiveness for my teenage nastiness, nor had I ever told him how much I truly cared about him.

Because I was the older of the two, I had my driver's license and drove us from our country farm into town to attend the local school. Whenever there were any special events at night or on the weekends, I was also the one who took us there. Some of the most vivid memories that stalked my mind after Don's death were about those experiences. I remembered how much I relished holding power over my younger brother, making him push me out of the snow, forcing him to beg for a ride someplace, and enjoying the ability to make him grovel for any of my driving services.

Don and I actually got along okay except for my holding the car keys. He never yelled at me, called me names, or held a grudge. When I moved on from high school and went on to college, though, we didn't see much of one another. Then he graduated and joined the army. While on duty in Europe, he fell in love with a woman who had a young son out of wedlock. They married and returned to the United States, but his wife and the child he had grown to dearly love eventually left him.

The last time I saw Don alive was shortly after this devastating divorce. I can still picture him clearly. He was sitting on a large sofa across from me, feeling depressed and dejected. I looked at his handsome face, his deep blue eyes, thinking what a good heart he had, what a kind and gentle person he was. After his death, each time this memory of our last visit arose, I would chide myself, "Why, oh, why, didn't I go over and hug him? Why didn't I try to comfort him? Why didn't I tell him what a neat guy I thought he was? Why didn't I let him know I loved him?" On and on the questions of regret hounded me, until I felt like I would cave in to their loud voices and cry forever. There was so much I wanted to undo, but could not. There was equally so much I wished I would have done, and had not. At the same time, I knew there was no changing the past.

This sort of guilt and self-recrimination went on for over a dozen years. Each time I tried to talk about my brother's death, I'd start getting tearful. This response told me I had not yet released the feelings I felt about the past, but I seemed unable to move beyond my mental and emotional struggle. Finally, I sought out a skilled counselor. She listened compassionately to my pain about Don's death and suggested that I try communicating with him in a written dialogue. I didn't really know how to do that but I decided, at that point, I'd try anything that might help free me from my sorrow.

I began my dialogue by addressing Don and pouring out a lot of words and emotion, naming the incidents that plagued me and everything I regretted doing. I ended by telling him how sorry I was for what I had done. Then I sat quietly for quite a while, trying to hear what he might say to me in response.

After some time, I picked up my pen and started writing again. What happened astounded me. It was one of the most freeing moments of my life. As I wrote Don's reply to me, these words came forth on the paper: "You silly, silly sister. I've forgiven you long ago. We were just high school kids. Stuff like that happens. The problem is, you've never forgiven yourself for how you treated me. Don't you think it's time?"

Those words assured me that any hurt I caused my brother had been dissolved. His message also named exactly what I needed to do. From that moment onward, I began to let go of my guilt and regrets. Every time I felt sad about what I had done to Don, I reminded myself that I was no longer a high school student. I was an adult woman who had grown and changed. I loved my brother and cared deeply about him. Gradually, I was able to put the past behind me. What helped me most to find peace were the words from the written dialogue. I returned to that paper often, hearing Don tell me that he had forgiven me long ago and that the rest was up to me.

Meditation

Select an experience that you deeply regret or feel guilty about when you think of your loved one who has died. Imagine that this person is with you now. Tell your loved one what troubles you and causes you to feel bad. Look into his (her) eyes. There is a glow of love there. You see complete kindness, mercy, and forgiveness pouring forth from him (her) to you.

Now he (she) speaks to you: "I love you. I forgive you for any hurt you may have done. Please forgive yourself." Hold this message in your heart and repeat it to yourself several times.

Close by visualizing the two of you embracing and being at complete peace with one another.

Prayer

Merciful One,
how I wish I could undo my faults and failings,
but the past is gone and cannot be regained.
Please accept my remorse for deliberate wrongdoing
and free me from whatever keeps peace away.

I turn to you with confidence in your mercy
and in hope of shedding the guilt that burdens me.
You know the sorrow and regret that I carry.
Teach me how to let go and forgive myself.
I will put the past behind and walk forward in love.

For Today

I will allow myself to be forgiven.

CHAPTER TWENTY-FIVE

What If I Forget

What You Looked Like?

BY SUSAN M.

I was fifty-five when my husband John became ill. We had fallen in love and stayed in love during our thirty-five years of marriage. His diagnosis of lung cancer dealt both of us a great blow. John struggled for two-and-a-half years with this disease. During this time, he received constant chemo and radiation therapy. Sometimes he had bouts of extreme weakness and needed to be mostly confined to bed. John also had some good intervals when his energy returned. In those periods of feeling better, he was more active and entered into a regular routine of daily life.

During the last six weeks of John's life, he remained in our home where he was cared for with hospice help. I continued to work full time in order to pay our bills but I spent every minute I could with my wonderful husband. John's mom and dad were excellent caregivers and a tremendous help to me. Thank goodness they lived close by and could often come during the day to check on John. Our two daughters, who lived out of town, took turns coming home for a week or two at a time when they were needed to help with their dad's care.

John's health condition changed significantly on a Sunday afternoon and we knew then that he was nearing death. We have a large extended family and a lot of our relatives stopped by to say goodbye to him. Our daughters, John's parents, and I were with him until he took his last breath on Tuesday night. Although I felt numb inside, I managed to get through the funeral and give my energy to what I had to do. Everything went as well as it could, but I felt completely drained as I said a final farewell to my dear husband. I couldn't imagine life without the person I loved with all my heart.

When my daughters returned to their homes, I went back to work in spite of constantly feeling depressed and lonely. I found coming home to an empty house the toughest part of each day. One of the things that helped me grieve was being able to talk to others about my loneliness and the many things I missed about John. I also spent a lot of time with his family and that softened my heartache because I knew they understood my sorrow.

After a year and a half, just about the time I thought I was moving beyond my loss and finally getting a grip on my life again, panic set in. I had this horrible thought: "What if I forget what John looked like?" The possibility that I could not remember his face, or be able to recall the loving way he had looked at me, caused me the greatest anxiety. I worried constantly that I'd wake up one day and not have any memories of him left. Each time I felt myself starting to feel better, I'd stop myself from doing so out of fear that I'd lose a sense of John completely.

I spent a lot of time looking at photos of John. This took the edge off of my anxiety because then his face was vividly clear and alive. I'd feel okay for a while but this release from worry was only temporary. The old panic returned soon after I put the photos away. A few days later, I would try to picture his face in my mind and again find only a blank space there. Although I dreamed about John during the first few months after he died, those dreams stopped coming. This added to my concern that I would forget him and no longer believe how much I loved him. John had always been my best friend, and now, there I was, not even able to remember what he looked like.

I found someone I felt comfortable with and con-
fided in her about my anxiety. The advice she gave
me really helped. She encouraged me to give up worrying about forgetting John's face and suggested
changing the focus of my memory. She was right. It
worked better for me to recall something John and I
had done together rather than try to recall his face.
This, in turn, helped me to picture him better. When I
thought about past events, I could remember special
things like John's laugh, the way he put his arm
around me, or the tall way he walked. Sometimes it
was a memory of spending a holiday or a vacation that
allowed me to remember what he looked like. After a
while, I realized that fear had been paralyzing my
mind and keeping me from forming a mental image of
the man I loved.

Something else that helped me get over my anxiety was a conversation I had with a friend. When I
explained how worried I was about not remembering
John's face, she told me about her brother who died
when they were both quite young. She had been
unable to remember his face for a long time. What
added to her confusion was trying to picture him at
the age he would currently be, rather than the age he
was when he died. She eventually realized she had to
quit worrying about it and let go of trying to find "a
face" for her brother.

My friend then shared how this problem finally
resolved itself: "One day I went to a movie and one of

the actors reminded me of my brother when he was young. In that moment, I 'saw' my brother's face. I was thrilled, even though I also experienced a sad tug at my heart because I had not seen him for such a long time. I also felt joyful because I realized that my mind was still capable of holding an image of what he looked like."

I gradually cast aside my fear of losing my memory of John, and now I trust the strength of my love for him. I know, too, that it's okay if I do not have a perfectly clear image of him in my mind. Photos do help keep alive my memory of him. Allowing my mind to bring forth whatever recollection of John that it wants to seems to work best for me. This keeps me from being overtaken with anxiety about picturing his face. I'm convinced now that I don't need to worry if I will ever be without a remembrance of him. My husband will always be a part of my heart. Love is stronger than death, and love most definitely is greater than a face that I am sometimes unable to recall.

Meditation

In Isaiah 49:15–16, God speaks: "I will not forget you. I have inscribed you on the palms of my hands." Reflect on the constant love the Holy One has for you, how deep and enduring this love is.

Now call to mind the vast love you have for the person you long to remember. Repeat several times the following adapted words of scripture to your dear one: "I will not forget you. I have inscribed you on my heart."

Sit quietly with this truth and let it sink deeply into you.

Prayer

Source of All Memories,
when I pause to picture the face of _____,
my heart fills with grateful remembrance.
Thank you for the beauty of our love.
I worry that one day I might forget,
not only physical looks, but all that I cherish.
When this fear and concern disturb me,
calm me with the grace of your abiding peace.
Assure me that my love for _____ will endure
and that this treasure will be forever in my heart.

For Today

I will look at a photo of my loved one and remember how strong and enduring my love is for him (her).

BY JOYCE HUTCHISON

Six months after my husband Gary died, my daughter Julie was married. I ached to have him there with us. I felt the biggest hole in my heart. Gary's not being there hid behind every joy. Both of my sons were in the wedding party. When I saw Joe in his tuxedo, the person standing before me made me catch my breath. At that moment, he looked just like his dad did at our wedding thirty-two years earlier. There is no way to describe how incredibly lonely I felt all through that day, even in the midst of several hundred people. The only thing that helped me survive was a dream I had had the night before; a sweet surprise.

Other people have shared with me their dreams of loved ones and how much those dreams helped to ease their heartache. I longed to dream about Gary but didn't have a single dream about him until the night before Julie's wedding. I went to bed that evening begging God to please help me get through the event and be able to give her the support and happiness she needed and deserved.

The morning of the wedding I woke up early. I was in the bathroom brushing my teeth when I gasped. I suddenly realized Gary had died. My dream had been so vivid that I thought he was still alive. In the dream he had come to me, kissed me on the cheek, and said, "I love you, Joycie." That moment in my dream was so real and natural that when I awoke I had a sense he was still with me. I even put my hand to my cheek and touched it. I could feel right where Gary had kissed me. This is the most vivid, real-to-life dream I have ever experienced. In the dream Gary also said he would be with me. Throughout the day of Julie's wedding, anytime I thought I might cry, I touched my cheek on the spot where he had kissed me and felt confident that he was truly there.

Gary's touch on my cheek assured me that I still had a connection with the man who claimed my heart long ago. Remembrance of that moment in the dream continues to bless my life today. This memory sustains my belief that those we love never leave our lives completely. My relationship with Gary and the love that united us will always be a part of me, just as the love and memory of your loved one will remain with you.

The one you love has gone Home and is now at peace. As you gradually move beyond your grief, I encourage you to trust the bond of love that forever unites you with your loved one. None of us knows how the future will unfold, but I hope you will walk into what awaits you with confidence, trusting that you will be given what you need to heal from your loss. The compassionate grace of God is with you and will uphold you through whatever storms and struggles come. You have more inner strength than you know. Trust in your ability to survive and to move on from your grief. Be ready for new touches of love and joy in your life. Welcome your restored peace when it returns and walk forward with hope in your heart.

Blessing

BY JOYCE RUPP

May your circle of understanding and caring persons be many and may you allow them to support and sustain you in your sadness.

May you rest your heartache in the compassionate arms of God each day and find comfort from this Enduring Love.

May you welcome the tears you shed as friends of your soul, gifting you with an opening to release your pain.

May disappointment, anger, guilt, or any other hurts that cling to you be acknowledged and set free.

May you trust the hidden part of you where your resilience resides and remember often the inner strength your spirit contains.

May you find the balance you need between activity and quiet so you can be attentive to your grief.

May you be gentle and compassionate with yourself by caring well for your body, mind, and spirit.

May you believe in your ability to eventually heal from your loss, no matter how much loneliness or desolation you now experience.

May you have the necessary energy to focus on the details of life that must be done, in spite of how you feel.

May the day come when memories of your departed one bring you more comfort than sadness.

May the empty hollow in you grow less wide and deep as you receive touches of consolation and assurances of peace.

May you be healed from your grief and extend your compassion generously to others who hurt.

May you recognize when it is time for you to let go and move on, doing so when your grief has faded and you are ready to allow the past to be at rest.

May you trust that love is stronger than death and draw comfort from the bond that unites you with your loved one.